KS3 Science

Essential SATS Practice

It's packed with lots of nasty questions — because they're the sort you'll get in the exam.

They're organised by topic, so you can easily see the types of questions you might get on each area of the curriculum.

Practise getting these questions right and you'll sweat a lot less on the big day.

Contents

Published by Coordination Group Publications Ltd.

Contributors:
Jenny Bilbrough, Martin Chester, Jason Howell, Kate Manson, Becky May, Emma Singleton and James Wallis.

ISBN: 1-84146-285-3

Groovy website: www.cgpbooks.co.uk

With thanks to Ian Francis and Dominic Hall for the proofreading.
Jolly bits of clipart from CorelDRAW

Printed by Elanders Hindson, Newcastle upon Tyne

KS3 Physics

Essential SATS Practice

Levels 3-6

CGP

Answers

Contents

Published by Coordination Group Publications Ltd

Groovy website: www.cgpbooks.co.uk

Printed by Elanders Hindson, Newcastle upon Tyne.

Section One — Electricity and Magnetism

Page 1
1 (a) Conductors. (b) (i) Insulators. (ii) Plastic, paper, limestone.

(c) A, C.

(d) (i) We know the conclusion that **aluminium** does not conduct electricity is wrong because **aluminium** is a **metal** and all **metals** conduct electricity.

(ii) Two of the circuits had gaps in them. Electricity would not flow even if the material being tested was a conductor.

This question looks tricky but isn't. Imagine yourself doing the experiment. Why aren't the results the ones you expect?

Page 2
1 (a) A flow of charge / electrons.

(b) (i) (ii)

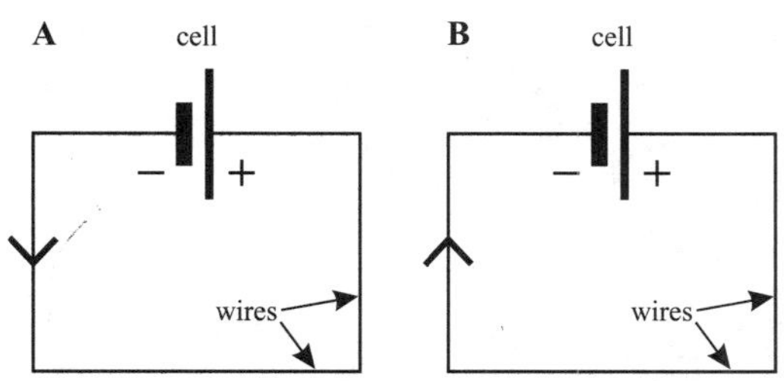

(c) (i) It pushes the charge around the circuit.

(ii) It completes the circuit. / It provides conducting materials all the way round the circuit. / It provides a path for the charge to follow. / It connects the positive and negative terminals of the cell.

(iii) It will increase.

Page 3
1 (a) The cell / battery is like a pump because it pushes the charge around the circuit.

(b) The wires are like the pipes because they connect the components in the circuit so the charge can flow around it.

(c) The current is like the water because it flows round the circuit.

(d) A bulb is like a narrow pipe because it creates resistance to the flow.

(e) In the same way that the water cannot be used up by the water system, charge cannot be used up by the electrical circuit.

Charge always exists, hidden away in particles. It just needs a push to get it to move.

Page 4
1 (a) (i) Bulb. (ii) Bulb. (iii) Cell. (iv) Battery.

(b) (i)

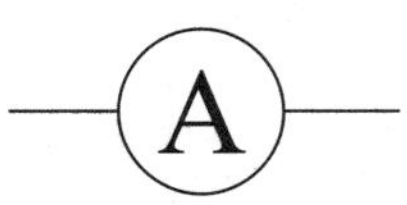

(ii)

2 (a)

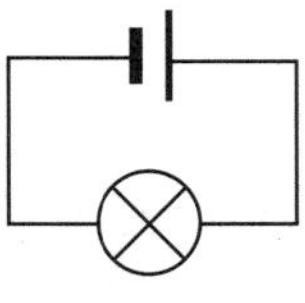

(b)

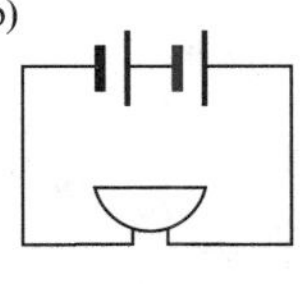

(c)

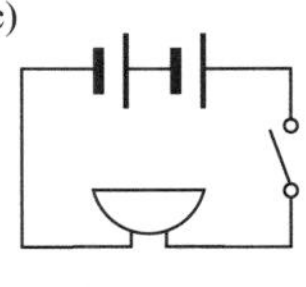

Draw any diagrams in the exam neatly, so you don't lose easy marks.

Page 5
1 (a) Amps / Amperes.

(b) Reading on A_2 **3 A**. Reading on A_3 **3 A**. It is a series circuit, and the current is the same everywhere in a series circuit. **or** The current can follow only one route so will be the same everywhere.

(c) Reading on A_1 **3 A** or **–3 A**. Reading on A_2 **3 A** or **–3 A**. Reading on A_3 **3 A** or **–3 A**.

(d) Reading on A_1 **0 A**. Reading on A_2 **0 A**. Reading on A_3 **0 A**. The circuit is broken / has no other route, so no current will flow.

Page 6
1 (a) From the charge / current.

(b) (i) It will be twice as bright. There is only one bulb, so resistance is halved / current is doubled.

(ii) 10.0 A. There are two cells instead of one, so compared to circuit 1 there is twice the force to push the current.

2 (a) It is shining with the same brightness as bulb A.

(b) (i) It will become very dim. **or** It will go out. (ii) A short circuit.

(c) It will become much brighter. There is much less resistance in the circuit. **or** It will shine twice as brightly. Resistance in the circuit is halved.

Page 7
1 (a) A circuit that branches. **or** A circuit in which the current can split / follow more than one route. **or** A circuit in which part of the circuit can be on when another part is off.

(b) (i) A_1 (ii) A_3

(c) A_1, because it shows the total current flowing through the circuit.

2 (a)

Ammeter	1	2	3	4	5
Reading (A)	8	2	5	**1**	**8**

(b) Ammeter **6** is faulty.

Page 8
1 (a) (i) A, D and E. (ii) A, C and E. (iii) A, B and E. (iv) A, B, C and E.

(b) (i) Closed. Both must be closed for current to flow.

(ii) It can be opened in an emergency. This will stop current flowing through the circuit.

(c) Connected in series the lights would all be on or off at the same time. In parallel, the lights can be turned on or off separately, so can be used to signal the traffic. **Accept** The lights will be brighter connected in parallel.

Page 9
1 (a) **Missing words in the following order** — cobalt / steel, steel / cobalt, a force.

(b) (i) They will line up along the field lines.

(ii)

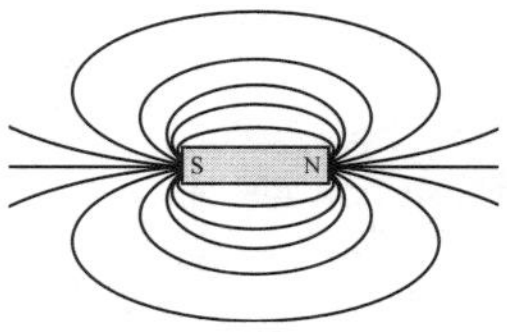

Accept arrows on the field lines if they point north to south.

(c) Place a compass at various positions around the magnet. It will always point from north to south along the field lines.

Page 10
1 (a) Bars X and Z. These are the only two bars that are repelled by each other, and repulsion can only happen between two magnets.

(b) Bar W. It is attracted to both X and Z but not repelled by either, so it is magnetic but not a magnet. Iron is magnetic.

(c) Bar Y. The other bars are attracted to W and X but Y is not, so it is not magnetic. Copper is not magnetic.

(d) [S N] [N S] or [N S] [S N]

(e) [S N] [S N] or [N S] [N S]

Page 11
1 (a) (i) A solenoid. (ii) Iron. (b) B, D, F, C, G, A, E.

(c) They have the same shape of magnetic field.

(d) An electromagnet can be switched on and off, a permanent magnet cannot. **and** Electromagnets are stronger than permanent magnets.

Page 12
1 (a) Current in circuit A turns on the electromagnet. This attracts the iron lever, which rotates and pushes the contacts together, turning on the heater and fan.

(b) (i) Circuit **B** is an input circuit. Circuit **A** is an output circuit.

(ii) The input of pressing the switch gives the output of the motor turning on.

(c) (i) A relay.

(ii) It uses a small current to switch on a large current in the drier circuit. **or** There is no electrical connection between the two circuits, so the larger current in circuit A cannot give the user a shock.

Page 13
1 (a) (i) 3 A

(ii) The current splits between the bulbs. Since the bulbs are identical, the same current flows through each one.

(b) No. The readings on ammeters A_1 and A_6 are the same.

2 (a) Yes. Repulsion is not possible without more than one magnet.

(b)

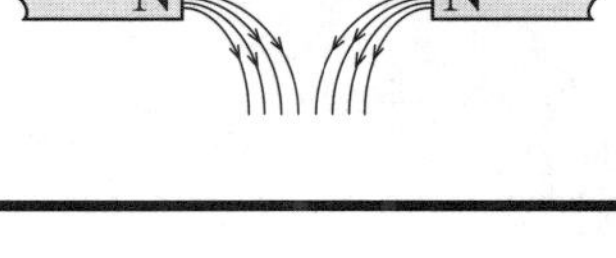

Page 14

3 (a) (i) A solenoid.

(ii) It is a good electrical conductor.

(iii) Plastic. **Accept** Rubber.

(b) An electromagnetic switch.

(c) (i)

A **This pushes the contacts together,** **turning on electromagnet B.**

B **The lever is attracted to electromagnet A,** **turning on electromagnet A.**

C **The switch is closed by the surgeon,** **and rotates towards it.**

(ii) 1 **C** 2 **B** 3 **A**

Page 15

3 (d) **The field lines should be shown with arrows pointing from one pole to the other, in either direction, e.g.**

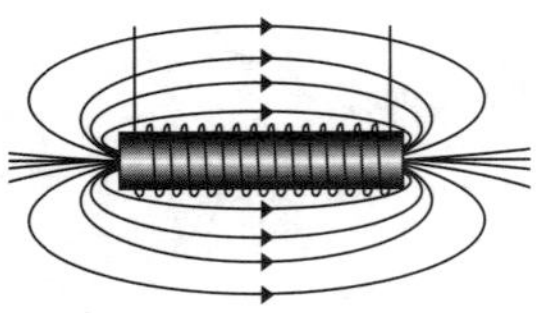

(e) (i) Steel, nickel. (ii) Steel and nickel are magnetic. The other metals in the list are not.

(f) It can be switched off until it is in the right position. **or** It is stronger than a permanent bar magnet.

Page 16

4 (a) In series.

(b) (i) A wire / connection that gives current a route of much lower resistance to flow round.

(ii) It will become twice as bright.

(iii) The resistance of the circuit has been halved.

(c) (i) It is a series circuit. / The bulbs are connected in series. / The circuit is either on or off. / The current is the same everywhere in the circuit.

(ii) **The bulbs and switches should be connected in parallel, e.g.**

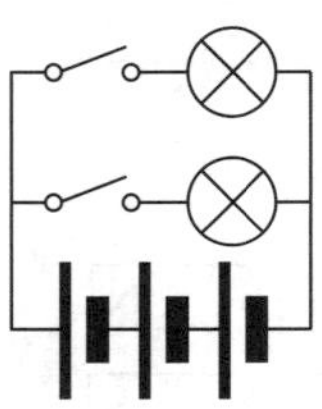

Section 2 — Forces and Motion

Page 17

1 (a) s = d/t = 150/100 = 1.5 m/s

(b) t = d/s = 150/2 = 75 s
Time difference = t on Monday – t on Tuesday = 100 – 75 = 25 seconds

This is a sneaky question. You don't just have to work out the time taken — you also have to work out the difference in the times taken.

2 (a) Because Clive's speed changed during the ride.

(b) Distance of ride = s × t = 24 × ¾ = 18 km.

Page 18

1 (a) s = d/t = 540/4 = 135 km/h

(b) (i) d = 540 × 1000 = 540 000 m (ii) t = 4 × 60 × 60 = 14 400 seconds

There are 60 mins in an hour, so there must be 60 times as many minutes. Same for seconds. So to get seconds from hours, multiply by 60, then multiply by 60 again.

(iii) s = d/t = 540 000/14 400 = 37.5 m/s

2 **Mark** d = s × t = 36 × 1 = 36 km
Corin d = s × t = (2 × 60) × 1 = 120 km
Jodie d = s × t = (1.8/1000 × 60 × 60) × 1 = 6.48 km **or**
d = s × t = (1.8 × 60 × 60) × 1 = 6480 m

Page 19

1 (a) Through liquid B.

(b) d = 50 cm = 50/100 m = 0.5 m
s = d/t = 0.5/5 = 0.1 m/s

(c) t = d/s = 0.5/1.0 = 0.5 s

(d) t = d/s = 15/2.5 = 6 s

(e) d = s × t = 0.4 × 23 = 9.2 m

Page 20

1 (a) The balloon will rise higher. (b) The balloon will get lower.

(c) The balloon will stay at the same height.

2 (a) (i) A newton meter. **or** A force meter. (ii) Newtons **or** N.

(b) (i) They are equal. (ii) They are opposite.

Page 21

1 (a) (i) **C** and **F** (ii) In C, the car is moving. In F, the boat is not moving.

(b) (i) E (ii) G (iii) D (iv) B (v) A

Page 22

1 (a) **Any two from —**
It allows her to grip the javelin. It allows her to run. It allows her to stop.

(b) (i) Air resistance / drag (ii) It will decrease.
(iii) It is opposite to the direction of flight.

(c) It would go further.

Page 23

1 (a) As the skydiver falls, her speed increases. This causes air resistance to increase.

(b) (i) It increases a lot. (ii) Air resistance and weight become equal / balanced.

(c)

	Diagram	Label
1	Z	C
2	V	E
3	Y	B
4	X	A
5	W	D

2 (a) A (b) B. It causes more air resistance so needs more energy to overcome it.

Page 24

1 (a) (i) (ii)

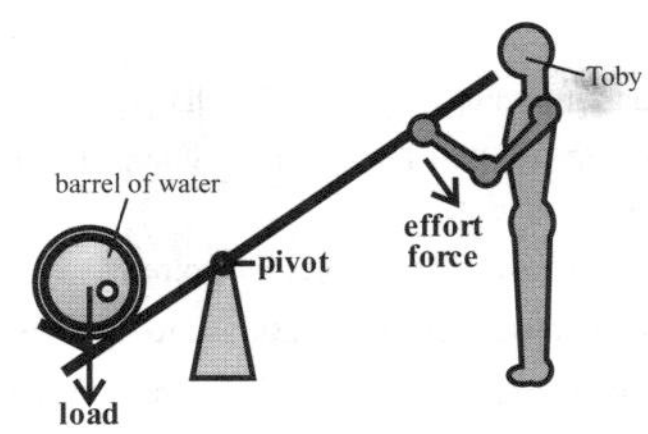

(b) The point that a lever rotates around.

(c) **Missing words in the following order —**
turning, size, distance, greater, leverage, smaller.

Notice that there are more words to choose from than gaps to fill.

Page 25

1 (a) (b) (c) (i) **The load arrow should point vertically downwards and the effort arrow should be at about 90º to the handle, e.g.**

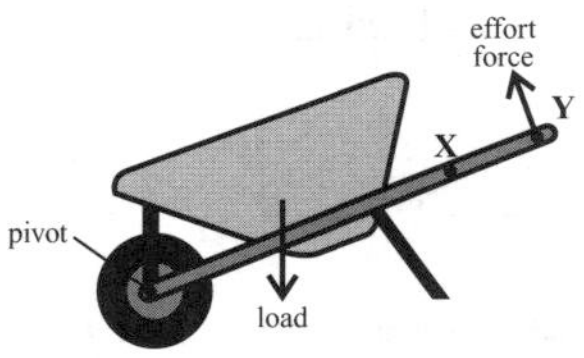

(c) (ii) Applying the force at Y gives a greater distance between the force and the pivot, so the turning force will be larger.

2 (a) A (b) **Any one from —**
The distance from the effort to the pivot will be longer.
The distance from the pivot to the load is shorter.

Page 26

1 (a)

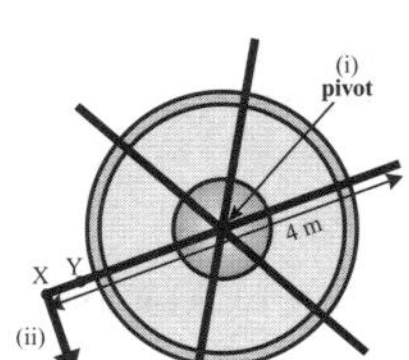

(b) (i) A moment. (ii) 4/2 = 2 m (iii) M = F × r = 80 × 2 = 160 Nm

You might be more used to seeing d for distance in the formula for calculating a moment, but r is sometimes used, too — r for the radius of the circle that (in this case) Ruth would walk in if she pushed the roundabout all the way round.

(c) More difficult. The distance from the pivot to the force is smaller, so she will have to push harder / exert more force to get the same turning effect.

Page 27

1 (a) They are opposite. **or** The rice creates a clockwise moment and the mass creates an anticlockwise moment.

(b) M = F × r = 10 × 0.25 = 2.5 Nm (c) M = F × r = 5 × 0.5 = 2.5 Nm
Yes. The moments are equal and opposite.

(d) For the mass: M = F × r = 5 × 0.1 = 0.5 Nm
For the rice: F = M/r = 0.5/0.25 = 2 N **or**
M = F × r
0.5 = F × 0.25
F = 0.5/0.25 = 2 N

Page 28

1 (a) Because this is the perpendicular distance of the weight from the pivot.

(b) M = F × r = 10 N × 0.3 m = 3 Nm **or** M = F × r = 10 N × 30 cm = 300 Ncm

(c) (i) It will get larger. (ii) It will get smaller.

(iii) As the pendulum moves toward the top of its swing, the perpendicular distance increases so the moment increases. As it moves toward the bottom of its swing, the perpendicular distance decreases so the moment decreases.

Page 29

1 (a) P = F/A = 20/0.8 = 25 N/cm^2

Pascals are N/m^2, so careful not to call these units Pascals. If you can remember that 1 Pascal is 1 N/m^2, then it gives you the formula for pressure.

(b) P = F/A = 20/0.01 = 2000 N/cm^2

(c) The sharper pin will have a point with a smaller area.
When pushed with the same force, it will exert more pressure on the wall.

2 (a) P = F/A = 450/0.06 = 7500 Pa **or** N/m^2. Anne is correct — it will sink.

(b) It will spread the force over a larger area.

Page 30

1 (a) F = P × A = 12 000 × 0.06 = 720 N

(b) 24 000 Pa **or** N/m^2. The area that Max's weight acts over is halved, so the pressure on the ice doubles.

(c) When he walks, the pressure he exerts on the ice will vary, depending on how much of his feet are in contact with the ice. **Also accept:** Whilst walking, the force he exerts will sometimes exceed his weight.

2 (a) F = P × A = 4 × 9 = 36 N (b) A = F/P = 28/4 = 7 cm^2

Page 31

1 (a) F = P × A = 29 000 × 7.25 = 210 250 N

(b) Maximum weight = maximum total weight – weight of foundations
= 210 250 – 58 000 = 152 250 N

2 (a) It will increase the area of the tyres in contact with the ground, reducing the pressure of the truck on the ground and making it less likely to get stuck.

(b) A = F/P = 24 000/40 000 = 0.6 m^2
Difference in area = 0.6 – 0.4 = 0.2 m^2

Page 32

1 (a) (i) The cyclist / bike moving through the air. **or** The air.

(ii) **Any one from —**
It allows the tyres to grip the road.
It allows the brakes to grip the rim of the wheel.
It allows the cyclist to grip the bike.
It holds together parts of the bike fixed by screws, nuts and bolts, etc.
Or any other sensible answer.

(b) No. The forces acting on him are balanced.

(c) s = d/t = 160/12.5 = 12.8 m/s

(d) **The following words should be crossed out —**
smaller, balanced, decreases, decreases, unbalanced, lower

Remember, air resistance increases as speed increases.

(e) s = d/t, t = d/s = 160/14.8 = 10.8 seconds

Page 33

2 (a) P = F/A = 27/(3 × 20) = 27/60 = 0.45 N/cm^2 **or**
P = F/A = 27 × 4/(3 × 20) × 4 = 108/240 = 0.45 N/cm^2

(b) P = F/a = 27 × 4/27 × 20 = 108/540 = 0.2 N/cm^2
Difference in P = 0.45 – 0.2 = 0.25 N/cm^2

(c) (i) M = F × r = 108 × 0.2 = 21.6 Nm. Yes.

(ii) Move the books closer to the wall, making the distance from the weight to P smaller, so making the moment smaller.

Page 34

3 (a) (i)

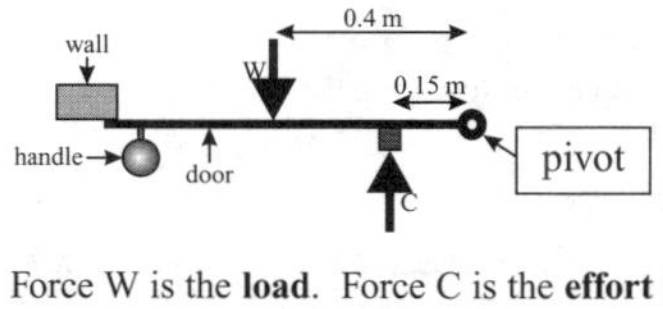

(ii) Force W is the **load**. Force C is the **effort force**.

Don't be put off by complicated-looking diagrams. Take your time to read through the information at the start of a question slowly and carefully, maybe more than once, and you'll find it's not really complicated after all.

(b) (i) A = 0.8 × 2 = 1.6 m^2 (ii) P = F/A, F = P × A = 20 × 1.6 = 32 N

Remember, area = length x width. Some tricky changing of the subject of the formula here, but if you can remember that pressure is force per unit area you can make a formula triangle. Or you can work it out from first principles — if there are 20 N of force for every m^2, then there must be 1.6 x 20 N altogether.

(c) (i) M = F × r = 32 × 0.4 = 12.8 Nm

Page 35

3 (c) (ii) Yes. The anticlockwise moment produced by the wind is greater than the clockwise moment produced by the closing device so the door will move anticlockwise.

(d) M = F × r = 40 × 0.15 = 6 Nm (e) (i) 6 Nm
(ii) M = F × r, F = M/r = 6/0.75 = 8 N

(f) She is exerting a force further from the pivot than force C.

(g) (i) The door will open further. (ii) The door will close further.

Section 3 — Light and Sound

Page 36

1 (a) **The statement that should be ticked is** Back-to-front and upside down.

(b)

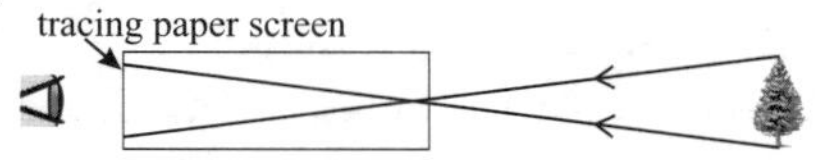

The pinhole camera demonstrates that light travels in straight lines. Use a ruler to draw straight rays, and put arrows on them to show what direction they're travelling in, and you'll pick up some easy marks.

(c) **The statement that should be ticked is** Light travels in straight lines.

Page 37

1 (a) **Missing words in the following order —**
luminous, travels directly, non-luminous, is reflected

(b)

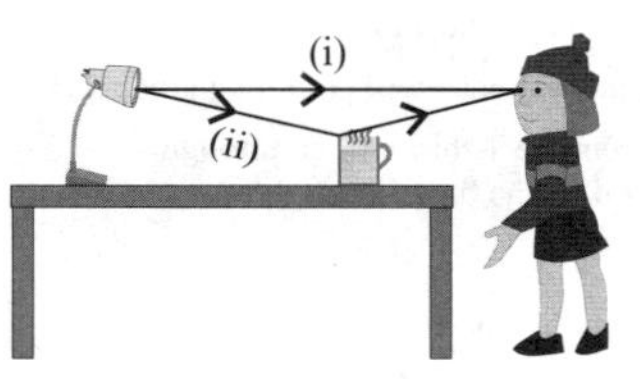

2 (a) They are luminous / produce light. (b) Light travels faster than sound.

Page 38

1 (a) It is reflected. (b)

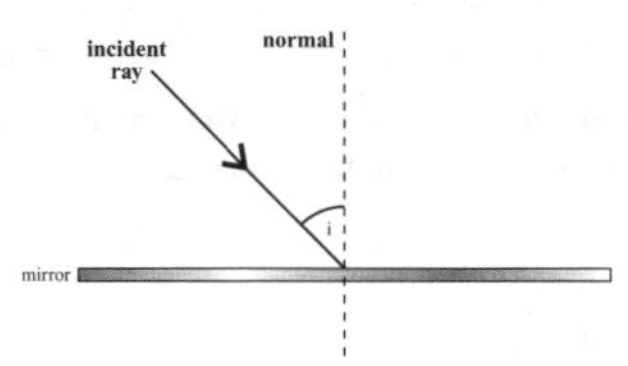

(c) (i) Angle i is the angle of **incidence**. (ii)

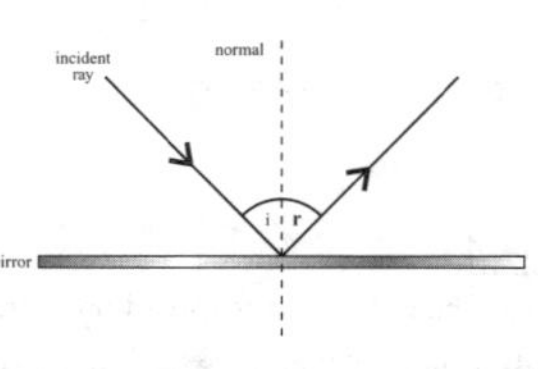

(d) (i) They are equal. **or** i = r (ii) A mirror has a smooth, shiny surface.

Page 39

1 (a) Yes (b) No. The rays would not come together.

Use a protractor to help you work out questions like this about angles of light rays.

(c) It will get larger. (d) (i) No. The rays of light are reflected at varying angles.
(ii) Diffuse.
(iii) **The statement that should be ticked is** It looks dull.

Page 40

1 (a) (i) **The statement that should be ticked is** They are transparent.

(ii) Refraction

(b) (i) **Missing words in the following order —**
towards, an angle, away from, a right angle.

(ii)

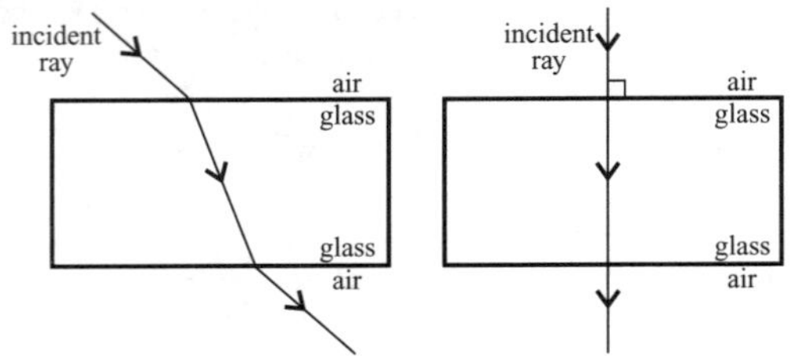

Page 41

1 (a) Its speed.

(b) Glass. The more light slows down, the more it will bend. The results show that it bends more when it enters the glass, so glass must be more dense.

(c) **The refracted ray should show that the light has bent towards the normal but only by a little, e.g.**

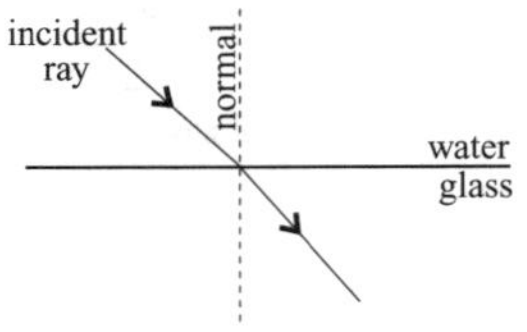

Page 42

1 (a) **Missing words in the following order** — dispersed, spectrum

(b) (i) Red (ii) Violet (iii) They are bent by different amounts.

(c) (i) The Sun. (ii) Rain / raindrops

Page 43

1 (a) (i) It reflects red light and absorbs all other colours.

(ii) They reflect blue light and absorb all other colours.

(iii) They reflect all colours of light.

(b) (i) Her T-shirt will look red because it reflects the red light.

(ii) Her jeans will look black because they absorb the red light.

(iii) Her trainers will look red because they reflect the red light.

(c) (i) Red. The red light reflected from the T-shirt will go through the filter.

(ii) Black. The red light reflected from the T-shirt will go through the red filter, but will be absorbed by the blue filter.

Page 44

1 (a) (i) **The term that should be ticked is** luminous

(ii) Before he switches it on, the light is reflected from the bulb. After, it comes directly from the bulb.

(b) (i) It is bent / changes direction. (ii) They are different.

Careful not to say that the gas is less dense than the glass. Even though this is probably correct, there's no evidence for it in the information given.

(iii) **The refracted ray should show that the light has bent away from the normal, e.g.**

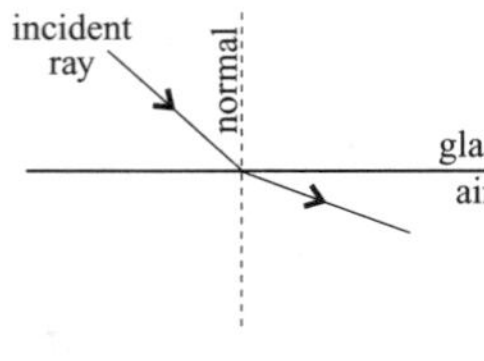

Page 45

1 (c) The colours in it spread out / are split up.

(d) White. White light is a mixture of all the colours in the spectrum, and a full spectrum appears on the screen.

(e) (i) No. Only red light can pass through the filter, and this is not a mixture of wavelengths like white light is.

(ii) Only red light.

(f) Because the red filter only lets red light through, but the blue screen only reflects blue light. It absorbs the red light, so no light can be seen on the screen.

Page 46

2 (a) (i) E (ii) F (iii) A

(b) (i) The incident ray. (ii) D. Angle of reflection = angle of incidence.

(iii) Light is reflected from the wood at varying angles. **or** Wood gives a diffuse reflection.

Page 47

1 (a) Sound travels more slowly than light. / Light travels much faster than sound.

(b) The sound travels as vibrations. **or** The sound waves carry energy.

(c) **Missing words in the following order** — energy, a medium, waves, vibration

2 (a) (i) It is reflected / bounces off the walls of the cave. (ii) An echo.

(b) Measure the time between the clap and its echo. Use the time and the speed of sound to calculate the distance the sound travels.

Page 48

1 (a) B (b) They are equally loud.

(c) **Any two from** — Ivan played the note more quietly. / Ivan was further from the microphone when he played the note. / Ivan changed the oscilloscope settings.

2 (a) (i) A (ii) B

(b) **The trace should look similar to the trace for quiet talking, but with a smaller amplitude, e.g.**

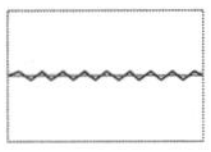

Page 49

1 (a) **Missing words in the following order** — complete, one second

(b) 1 a road drill 2 a car engine 3 a dentist's drill 4 a scream

(c) It will get higher-pitched / higher.

2 (a) A and D (b) A and C (c) B and D

Page 50

1 (a)

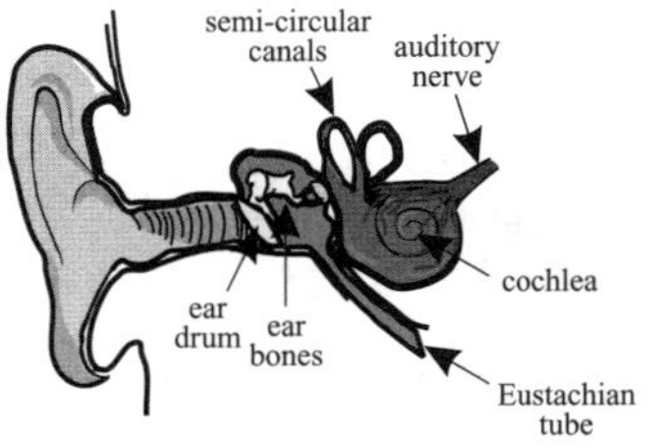

(b) The vibrations are passed from Julie's vocal chords to the air, to Heather's ear drum, then to her ear bones and on to her cochlea. Hairs in her cochlea vibrate, triggering the nerve cells of the auditory nerve. The signals are sent to Heather's brain.

(c) (i) Decibels (ii) **Any estimate in the range** 1–30.

(iii) The teacher is older than Julie. / Julie is younger than the teacher.

Page 51

1 (a)

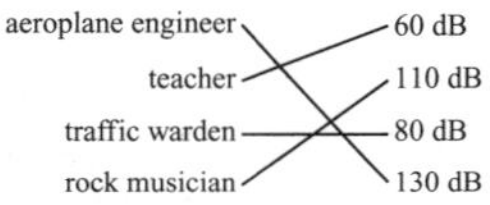

(b) The rock musician and the aeroplane engineer.

2 (a)

Animal	Audible range (Hz)
chicken	125 – 2000
bat	2000 – 110 000
porpoise	75 – 150 000
chinchilla	90 – 22 800
elephant	16 – 120 000

(b) Hertz

(c) They are difficult to find out. **and** Not every individual will have the same range. **Or any other sensible answer.**

Page 52

1 (a)

	60 dB	80 dB
8000 Hz	C	B
10 000 Hz	A	D

(b) (i) Frequency

(ii) Amplitude / loudness

(c) D (d) (i) B D C E A

(ii) The vibration of the hairs in the cochlea triggers auditory nerve cells, sending signals to the brain.

(e) The closer the clock is, the louder the alarm will sound.

Page 53

2 (a) (i) The sound of the watch would disappear. **and** The watch / image of the watch would disappear. / The bell jar would go dark.

(ii) The sound of the watch disappeared.

Don't get confused by the word 'observe' — it doesn't just mean what you'll see.

(b) (i) It will not travel in a vacuum. (ii) It will travel in a vacuum.

3 (a) (i) B (ii) C (iii) A

(b) The sound loses energy, so the amplitude of the wave decreases.

Section 4 — The Earth and Beyond

Page 54

1 (a) (i) The rotation of the Earth.

(ii) There is one complete rotation of the Earth.

(b) It is daytime in region B and night time in region C.

(c) **The statement that should be ticked is** The Sun has just set.

2 (a)

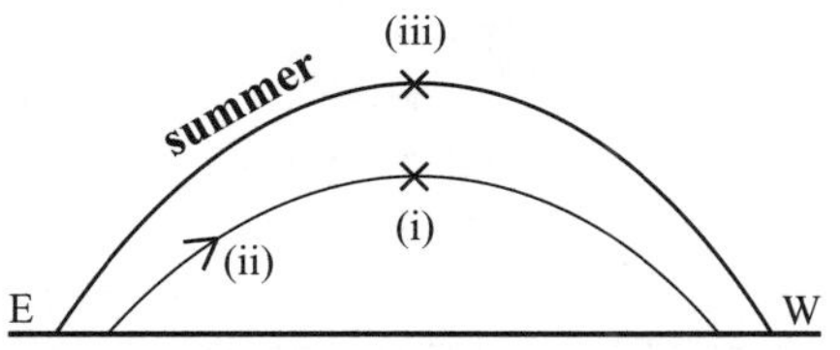

(b) During winter, because the Sun is lower at midday than during summer.

Page 55

1 (a)

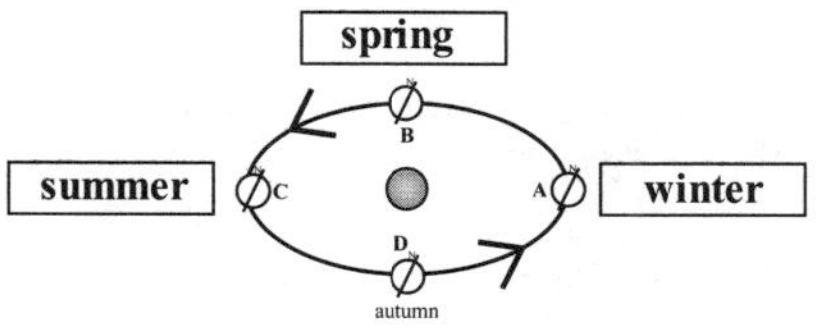

(b) 3 months

(c) **The following words should be crossed out** — shorter, larger, weakest, cold

(d) **The statement that should be ticked is**
The Earth's axis leans over at an angle of 23.5°.

Page 56

1 (a) **Missing words in the following order** — natural, an anticlockwise, twenty-eight

(b) (i) Light from the Sun. (ii) It reflects light from the Sun.

(c) (i)

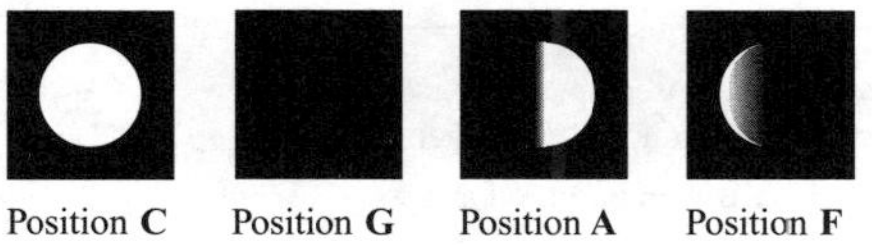

Position **C** Position **G** Position **A** Position **F**

(ii) Different amounts of the sunlit part of the Moon are seen.

Page 57

1 (a) Gravity (b) Larger. Zod is larger than the Earth so has more mass. The larger the mass, the stronger the force of gravity.

(c) Smaller. Ved is further from Zed than the Moon is from the Earth.
The larger the distance between objects, the weaker the force of gravity.

(d) (i) It will be the same.

(ii) It will be heavier. Zod has more mass than Earth, so there will be a stronger gravitational attraction between Zod and the probe.

Page 58

1 (a) **Any two from** — radio, television, telephone

(b) Fewer stations on the ground are needed. **or** The signal can be sent further.

(c) It stays above the same place on the Earth's surface.

2 (a) The Earth's atmosphere does not block the view.

(b) **Any one from** —
To monitor weather / track storms.
For mapping.
To monitor the Earth's atmosphere / the ozone layer.
To track ocean currents.
Or any other sensible answer.

Page 59

1 (a) (i) **From first to last:** Pluto Earth Neptune Jupiter Sun

This one might look a bit tricky at first, but fill in the bits you can work out, and it soon turns out nice — Pluto's the smallest, Jupiter's the biggest planet, and the Sun's bigger than everything else in the Solar System put together, so all these can be filled in. Choosing between Earth and Neptune is a bit more difficult, but all the outer planets apart from Pluto are pretty big (they're called 'gas giants').

(ii) Its large mass / size means it exerts a strong force of gravity.

(b) They reflect light from the Sun.

(c) (i) They are the closest planets to the Sun.

(ii)

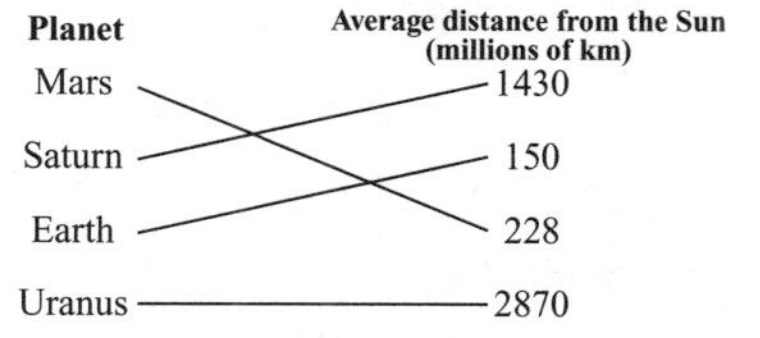

(d) **Any one from** —
moons, asteroids, comets, meteoroids / meteors / meteorites, dust.

Page 60

1 (a) They are compared to the size and mass of the Earth.
Accept They are compared to each other.

(b) (i) Venus (ii) Uranus (iii) Neptune

2 (a) The further a planet is from the Sun, the longer its orbit time. **or**
The closer a planet is to the Sun, the shorter its orbit time.

(b) **Any one from** —
They are circular instead of elliptical / not the correct shape.
They are not to scale / do not show the relative distances travelled.
Or any other sensible answer.

Page 61

1 (a) **From smallest to largest**: Earth, Sun, Solar System, a galaxy, Universe

(b) A collection of stars. (c) A small, blurred star.

(d) (i) The Milky Way (ii) Because they're so far from Earth.

Page 62

1 (a) **The term that should be ticked is** elliptical. (b) A year.

(c) **The Earth should be shaded so that the dividing line between the light and dark side is vertical, e.g.**

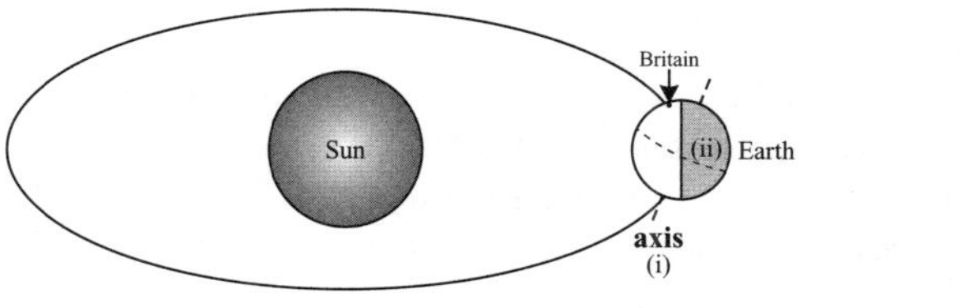

Remember, the Earth's axis and the day / night division are different lines.

(d) **The statements that should be ticked are**
The Sun rises and sets every day. **and**
The stars follow curved paths through the night sky.

Page 63

1 (e) (i) **The statement that should be ticked is**
Night time lasts longer than daytime.

(ii) Weakest. The North is tilted away from the Sun so the heat of the Sun's rays is spread out more than when it is tilted towards the Sun.

(iii) Winter

(iv) Summer. When the northern half of the Earth is tilted away from the Sun, the southern half is tilted towards it.

(f) **The term that should be ticked** much larger**.**

(g) (i) Venus, Mars. (ii) Venus is too hot. Mars is too cold.

Page 64

2 (a) **The following words should be crossed out** — second, twice, 225

(b) Asteroids / the Asteroid Belt

(c) An object that orbits around a planet. **Accept** An object in orbit.

(d) (i) Gravity (ii) The mass of Mars and its moons.

Don't forget that mass and size are different.

3 (a) (i) A star. (ii) Heat from the Sun.

(b) It will increase. The smaller the distance between objects, the stronger the gravitational attraction between them.

Page 65

4 (a) They are all very far away.

(b) (i) A galaxy. (ii) It contains many stars.

5 (a) B. It has a larger orbit, so takes most time to complete an orbit.

(b) Satellite **A** is likely to be the weather satellite because
it will pass over the surface of the Earth.

Satellite **B** is likely to be the television satellite because
it will stay above the same place on the Earth's surface.

0604 - 1667

Section 5 — Energy Resources and Energy

Page 66

1 (a) (i) Kinetic (ii) Elastic
(iii) Gravitational potential **(accept** kinetic) (iv) Light

(b)

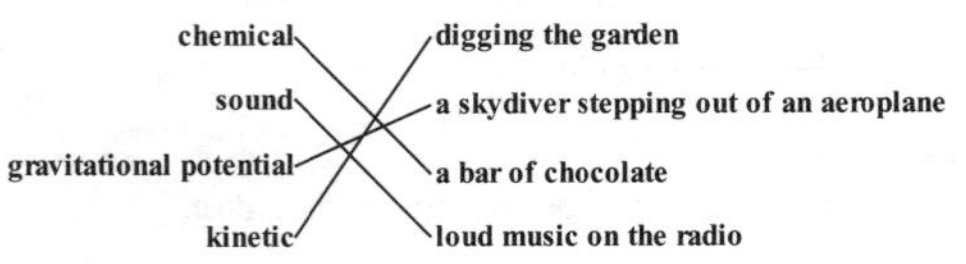

(c)

Component	Form of energy
Battery	**Chemical**
Wires	**Electrical**
Starter motor	**Kinetic**
Headlamp	**Light**
Radio loudspeaker	**Sound**

Page 67

1 (a) D (b) E (c) B (d) G

(e) Letter **A** Example **Any example of gravitational potential energy, e.g. A skier at the top of a slope.**
Letter **C** Example **Any example of chemical energy, e.g. A lump of coal.**
Letter **F** Example **Any example of elastic energy, e.g. A catapult ready to fire.**

Page 68

1 (a) Light (**accept** heat / thermal) → electrical
(b) Electrical → sound
(c) No. Some energy will be wasted. **or**
Some of the energy will be transformed into forms other than sound.

2 (a) Electrical to chemical **should be ticked.**
(b) Chemical to electrical to kinetic **should be ticked.**
(c) Sound **and** heat / thermal.

Page 69

1 (a) (i) Chemical (ii) From food. (iii) Kinetic
(b) (i) Kinetic (ii) Sound **and** heat / thermal.

2 (a) Gravitational potential to kinetic.
(b) Electrical to sound and light. **or** Electrical to sound and light and heat / thermal.

Page 70

1 (a) Photosynthesis
You should know about photosynthesis from the biology bits of your science lessons.
(b) (i) Food **or** wood **or any other sensible answer.**
(ii) Light energy from the Sun is converted into chemical energy by plants, which is converted into heat and kinetic energy when we eat the plants (or animals that have eaten the plants) as food. **or**
Light energy from the Sun is converted into chemical energy by trees, which is converted into heat energy when we burn their wood as fuel.
Or any other sensible answer.
(c) **The answer that should be ticked is** fossil fuels.

2 (a) Kinetic
(b) The Sun. Energy from the Sun heats up the atmosphere, causing winds.
(c) Wave power / waves

Page 71

1 (a)

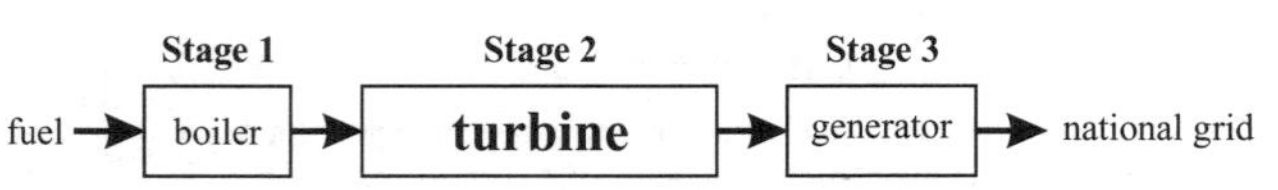

(b) (i) 3 (ii) 2 (iii) 1
(iv) 3 (v) 2 (**accept** 1) (vi) 1
(c) (i) Coal, oil **and** natural gas. (ii) It is too expensive.
(d) It delivers electricity to homes.

Page 72

1 (a) Fossil fuels are being used more quickly than they can be replaced.
(b) **The statement that should be ticked is**
Oil has many important uses other than generating electricity.
(c) (i) **Any two sensible ways of using less energy, e.g.** turning off lights, using energy-saving light bulbs, driving cars with lower fuel use.
(ii) **Any three from** — solar power, wind power, wave power, tidal power, hydroelectric power, geothermal power, biomass.

Page 73

1 (a) (i) Sound
(ii) It does not help the hair dryer to do what it is designed for. **or** It is an unintended result of converting the energy input into useful energy output.
(b) **The equation that should be ticked is**
heat energy + kinetic energy = energy input – wasted energy
(c) Energy cannot be destroyed / used up, only converted from one form to another.

Page 74

1 (a) The energy saver light bulb wastes less energy.
(b) **Any two from** — cheaper, uses less energy / saves energy, reduces use of fossil fuels, reduces pollution from electricity generation.

2 (a) (i) 25 (ii) 200 (iii) 320
(b) (i) Kinetic (ii) Electrical
(c) (i) The wind turbine. (ii) The lawnmower.
(d) Heat / thermal **and** sound.

Page 75

1 (a) (i) Chemical energy → electrical energy → kinetic energy
(ii) Gravitational potential energy
(b) (i) Gravitational potential energy to kinetic energy.
(ii) Kinetic energy → electrical energy → light energy
(iii) Heat
(c) It will be less. As it is transformed, energy is continually being lost. / Not all the energy is converted into useful forms.

Page 76

2 (a) (i) D (ii) Coal **and** natural gas.
(b) (i) A
(ii) **Any biomass energy resource, e.g.** food, biogas.
(c) (i) It is the original source of the energy in oil and wood.
(ii) It is the process plants use to convert light energy from the Sun to the chemical energy in wood and oil.
(iii) Wood can be used as an energy resource as soon as it has grown.
Oil takes millions of years to form /
is formed from the fossilised remains of plants / animals.

Page 77

2 (d) Light energy → chemical energy → heat energy
(e) (i) No. Energy cannot be used up, only converted from one form to another.
(ii) Yes. Once they have been burnt, oil and wood cannot be burnt again.
(f) (i) Trees can be grown quickly enough to replace the wood burnt.
Oil forms very slowly and cannot be replaced.
For this one, you need to explain <u>both</u> why wood is renewable <u>and</u> why oil is not.
(ii) It will run out. **or** It has important uses apart from providing energy.
(iii) **Any two from** — solar power, wind power, wave power, tidal power, hydroelectric power, geothermal power, biomass.

Page 78

3 (a) (i)

	Machine	Energy Transformation
A	generator	**kinetic to electrical**
B	**turbine**	heat to kinetic
C	boiler	**chemical to heat / thermal**

(ii) C B A
(b) (i) heat / thermal (ii) 16 J
(iii)

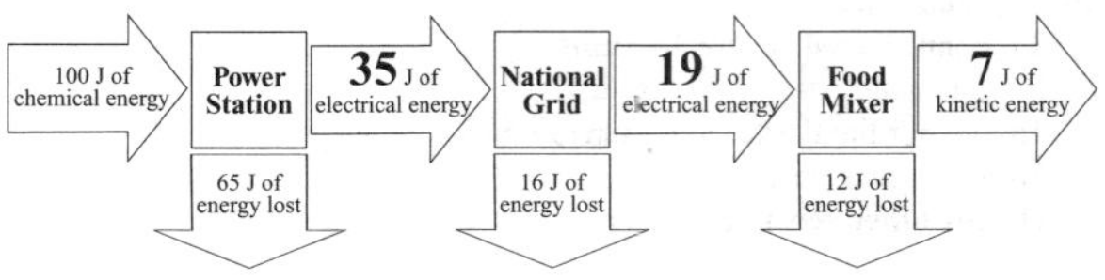

Electrical Conductors

1 In order to carry a current, a circuit must be made from materials which all allow electricity to flow through them.

(a) What name is given to materials that allow electricity to flow through them?

Conductors

(b) (i) What name is given to materials that electricity will **not** flow through?

insulators

(ii) Underline the materials in the list below that electricity will **not** flow through.

aluminium **plastic** **graphite** **paper** **steel** **limestone**

Nathan has set up a test circuit for identifying materials that electricity will flow through. Three of his tests are shown below.

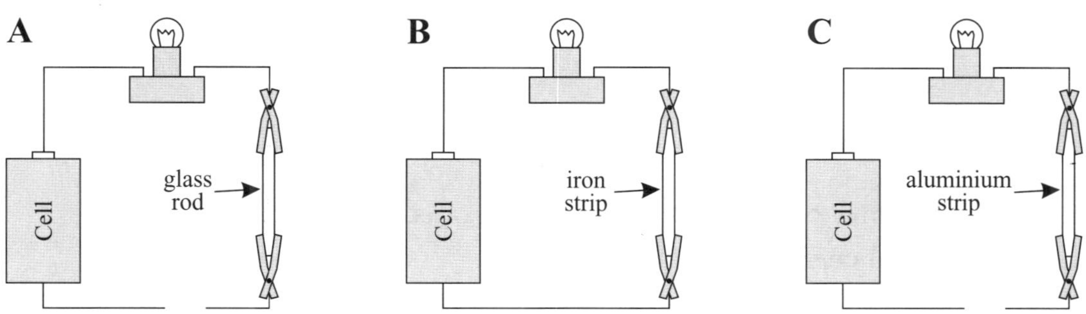

(c) In which circuits will the bulb **not** light? Write their letters here: A C

(d) From the evidence of the tests above, Nathan concludes that electricity will flow through iron, but not through glass and aluminium.

(i) Nathan's conclusion is not completely correct. Fill in the gaps in the sentences below to show why.

We know the conclusion that aluminium **does not conduct electricity is wrong because** aluminium **is a** metal **and all** metals **conduct electricity.**

(ii) Why was the evidence from Nathan's tests not reliable?

Two circuits had gaps in them. Electricity would not flow even if the material tested was a conductor

Electric Current

1 Both of the circuits below have an electric current flowing through them.

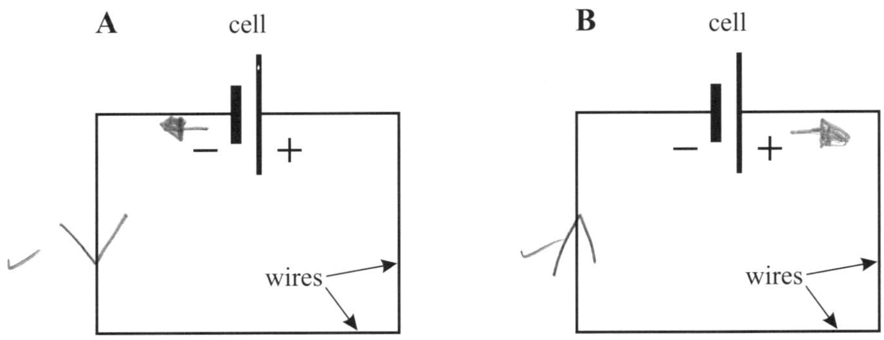

(a) What is an electric current?

A flow of charge / electrons

An electric current is the electcity flow through

(b) (i) Draw **one** arrow on circuit **A** to show which direction **charge** flows around it.

(ii) Draw **one** arrow on circuit **B** to show which direction **conventional current** flows around it.

(c) Each circuit shown above contains only a cell and a wire.
This is the smallest number of components needed for a current to flow.

(i) What does the cell do to make current flow round the circuit?

It pushes the charge around the circuit

(ii) What does the wire do to make current flow round the circuit?

It completes the circuit / Provides conducting materials all the way round / path for charge to follow

connects positive / negative terminals of cell.

(iii) A light bulb is added to each circuit.
What will happen to the **resistance** in the circuits?

It will increase.

Electric Current

1 An electrical circuit can be compared to a system of water pipes.

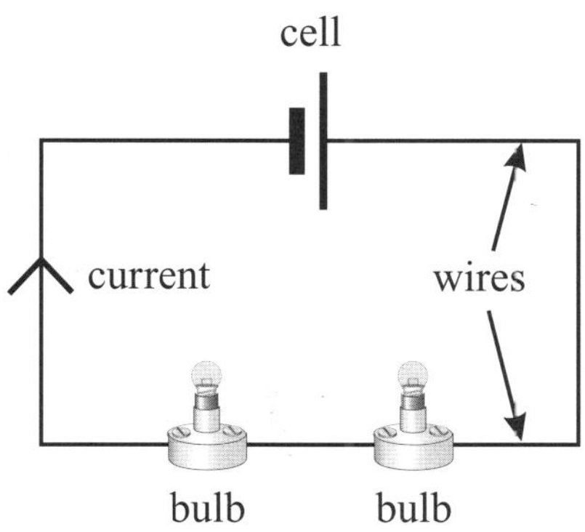

electrical circuit

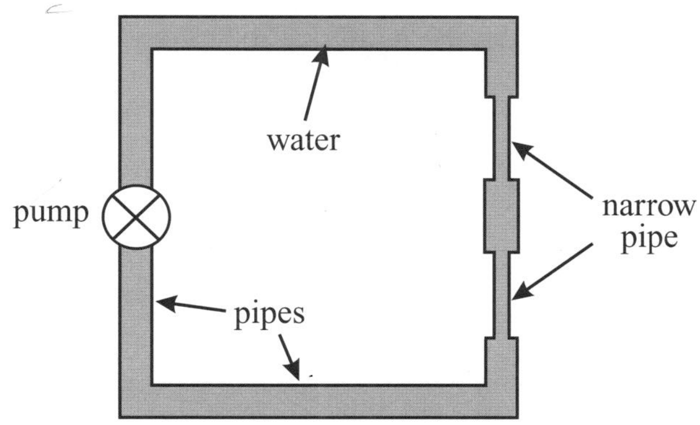

water system

Look at the two diagrams above. For each part labelled on the water system, give the equivalent part labelled on the electrical circuit, and explain why they are similar.

(a) **The** ......Cell...... **is like a pump because** ...it generates...

...electricity through there or * Pushes charge around circuit....

(b) **The** ......Wire...... **are like the pipes because** ...they...

...make the electricity flow, X * connect components in the circuit so charge can flow around....

(c) **The** ......Current...... **is like the water because** ...it flows...

* ...round the circuit...

(d) **A** ......bulb...... **is like a narrow pipe because** ...it creates...

* ...resistance to the flow...

Tamar is asked to explain what happens in the electrical circuit to make the bulbs light. She says "The cell pushes current round the circuit, and some of it is used in the bulbs to make light."

*

(e) Explain why Tamar's statement is incorrect by comparing the electrical circuit to the water system.

...Because she mentions about lights / bulbs...

...which are not present in a water system. X

* In the same way water cannot be used up by water system charge cannot be used up by electrical circuit.

Circuit Diagrams

1 Electrical components can be represented by symbols.

(a) Write down the names of the components with the following symbols.

(i)

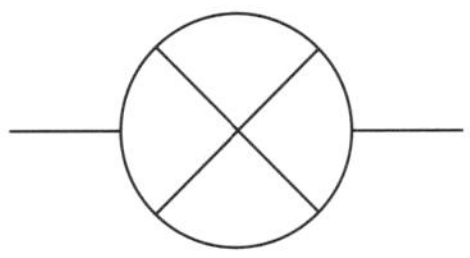

Bulb

(ii)

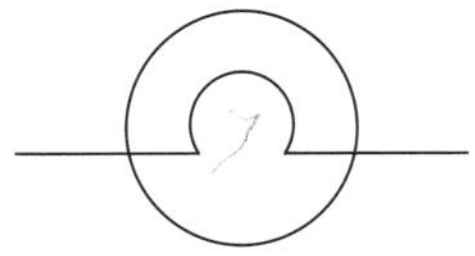

Bulb

(iii)

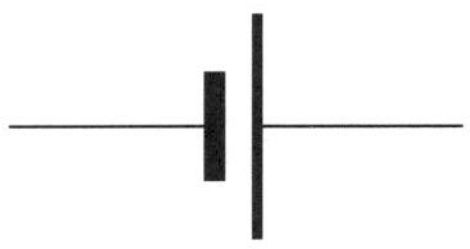

Cell

(iv)

Battery

(b) Draw the correct symbol for each of the following components.

(i) An ammeter.

(ii) A motor.

2 Electrical circuits can be represented by diagrams.
Draw a circuit diagram for each of the following circuits.

(a)

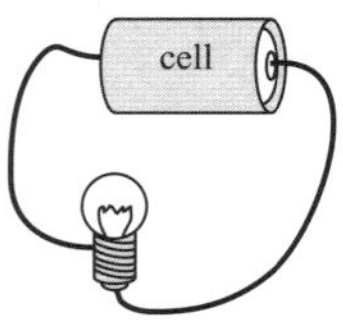

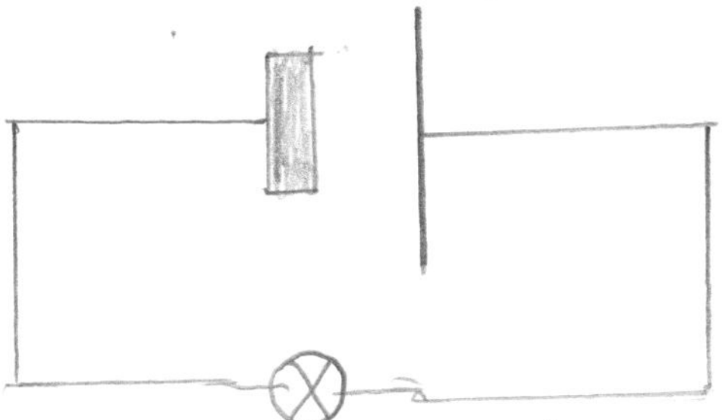

(b)

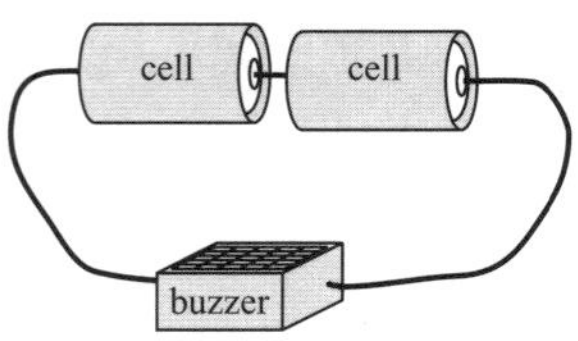

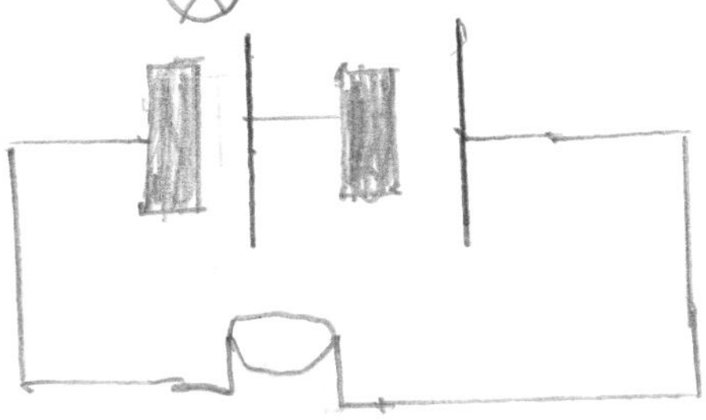

(c) A circuit with two cells, a buzzer and an open switch.

Series Circuits

1 An ammeter is an instrument that can be used to measure electric current.

(a) The unit used to measure electric current has the symbol **A**.
What does this symbol stand for?

Ammeter × Amps / Amperes

In a series circuit, the current can follow only one route.
The series circuit below contains three ammeters. The reading on A_1 is 3 A.

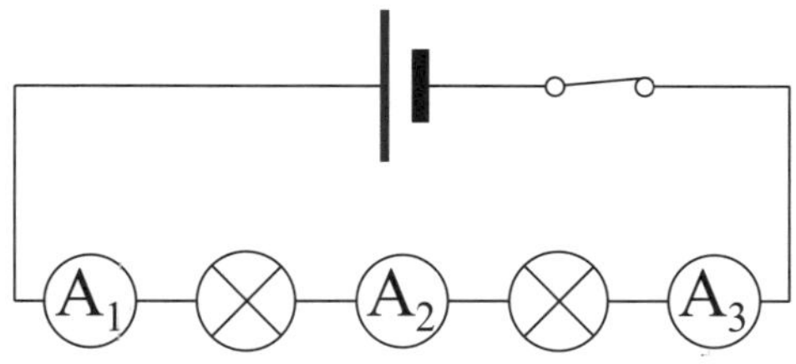

(b) What will the readings on A_2 and A_3 be? Explain your answer.

Reading on A_2 .... **Reading on A_3** ....

....

....

(c) The cell is disconnected from the circuit and reconnected with its terminals the other way round, as shown below.
Suggest what the ammeter readings will be now.

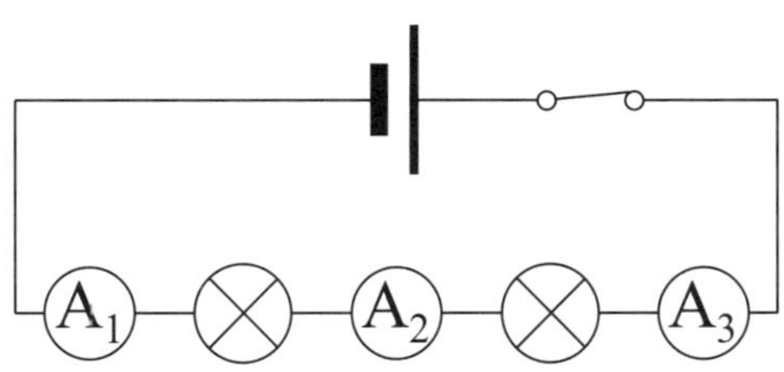

Reading on A_1 .... **Reading on A_2** .... **Reading on A_3** ....

(d) The switch is opened. What will the ammeter readings be now?
Explain your answer.

Reading on A_1 .... **Reading on A_2** .... **Reading on A_3** ....

....

....

Series Circuits

1 The circuits shown on the right contain identical cells and identical bulbs.
The bulbs in **circuit 1** are shining brightly.

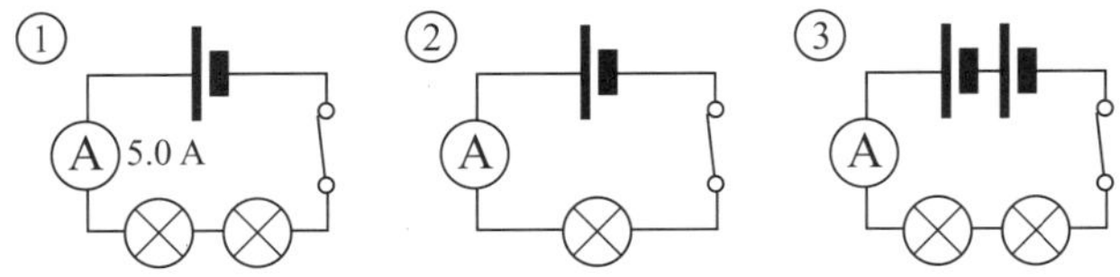

(a) Where does the light energy given out by the bulbs come from?

(b) (i) How will the brightness of the bulb in **circuit 2** compare with the brightness of the bulbs in circuit 1? Explain your answer.

(ii) What will the ammeter read in **circuit 3**? Explain your answer.

2 In the circuit on the right, one end of a piece of wire is connected between the two bulbs. The other end is loose.

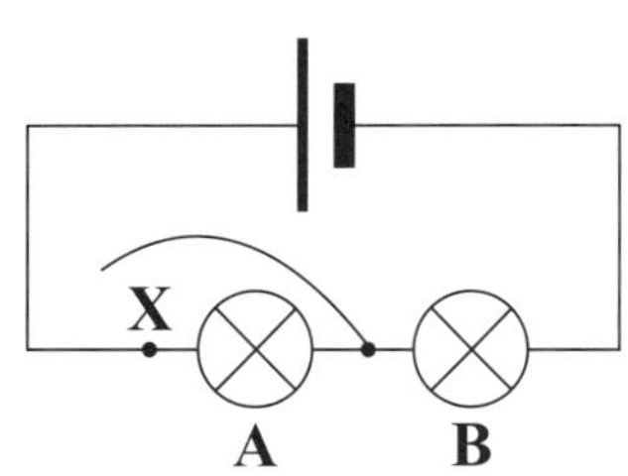

(a) Bulb A is shining brightly.
What can you say about the brightness of bulb B?

The loose wire is connected at point X.

(b) (i) What will happen to bulb A?

(ii) What is this type of connection called?

(c) What will happen to bulb B? Explain your answer.

Parallel Circuits

1 The diagram on the right shows a parallel circuit containing a cell, a bulb, a motor and four ammeters.

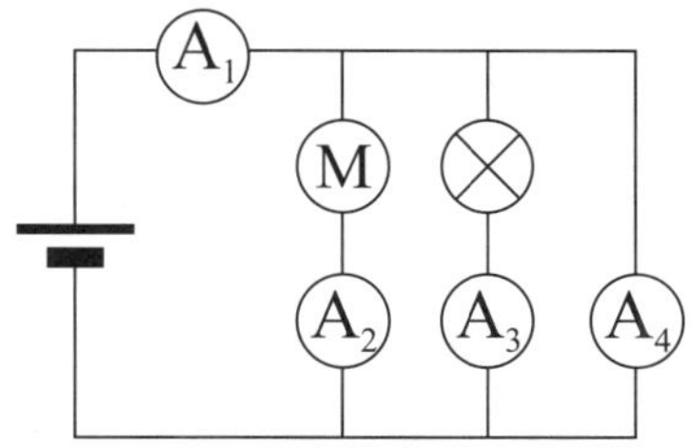

(a) Explain what is meant by a **parallel circuit**.

....

....

(b) (i) Which ammeter will show how much current, **in total**, is flowing through the circuit — A_1, A_2, A_3 or A_4? ....

(ii) Which ammeter will show how much current is flowing through the **bulb** — A_1, A_2, A_3 or A_4? ....

(c) Which ammeter would you expect to have the highest reading — A_1, A_2, A_3 or A_4? Explain your answer.

....

....

2 The parallel circuit shown on the right contains a cell, a motor, a bulb, a buzzer and five ammeters.

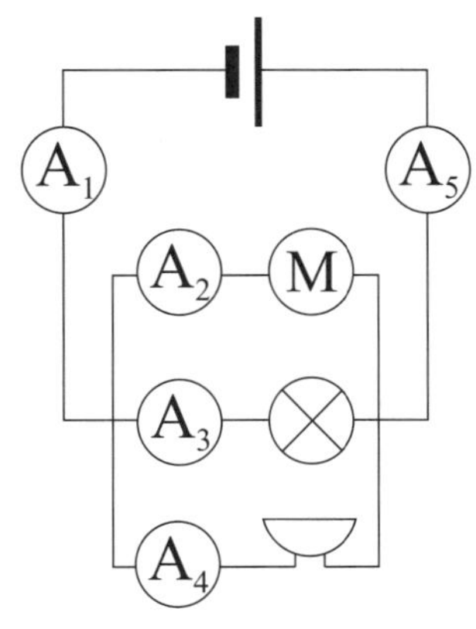

(a) Complete the table below to show all the ammeter readings.

Ammeter	1	2	3	4	5
Reading (A)	8	2	5		

(b) A new circuit (shown on the right) is set up, using five new ammeters and three different types of bulb. One of the new ammeters is faulty. Use the readings below to work out which one it is.

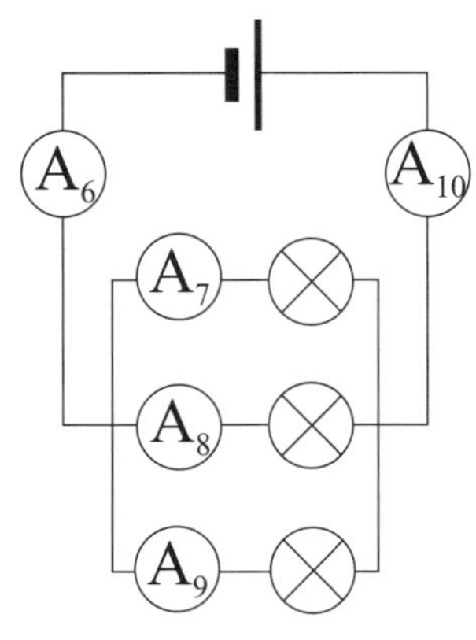

Ammeter	6	7	8	9	10
Reading (A)	9	3	5	2	10

Ammeter .... is faulty.

Parallel Circuits

1 Mobile traffic lights are sometimes used at roadworks. A simplified diagram of a circuit used for a set of mobile traffic lights is shown on the right.

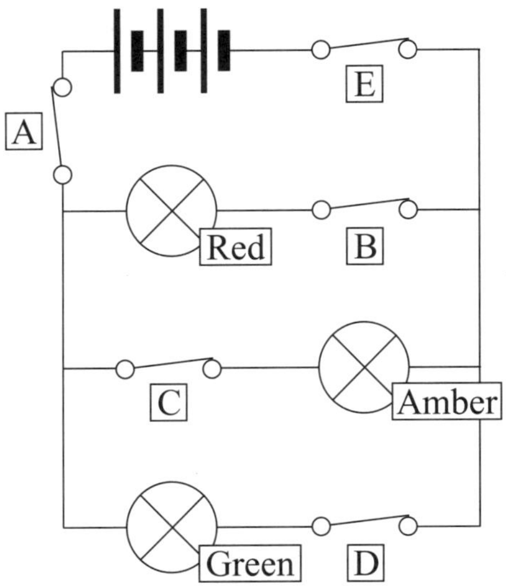

(a) List all of the switches **A** to **E** that must be closed for the signal to be

(i) green.

....

(ii) amber.

....

(iii) red.

....

(iv) red and amber.

....

(b) Switch **A** is used to switch on the traffic lights when the workmen begin work. Switch **E** is an emergency shutoff switch.

(i) When the lights are working normally, are switches A and E open or closed? Explain your answer.

....

....

(ii) Explain how switch E can be used in an emergency to shut off the current.

....

....

(c) Give **one** reason why the lights in the circuit above are connected in parallel and not in series.

....

....

Magnets

1 (a) Complete the following sentences about magnets by filling in the missing words. Choose from the list below.

repulsion **cobalt** **brass** **a force** **copper** **steel**

Iron, nickel, ...Steel...... **and** ......Cobalt......

are all magnetic. When placed in a magnetic field, objects made

from these materials will experience ......a force...... .

(b) Rhys is using iron filings to investigate the magnetic field around a bar magnet. He scatters the filings around the magnet.

(i) What will happen to the iron filings as Rhys scatters them around the magnet?

The iron filings will attract around the magnet. X They will line up along the field lines.

(ii) Rhys is using the diagram below to record his findings. Complete it to show the results he can expect.

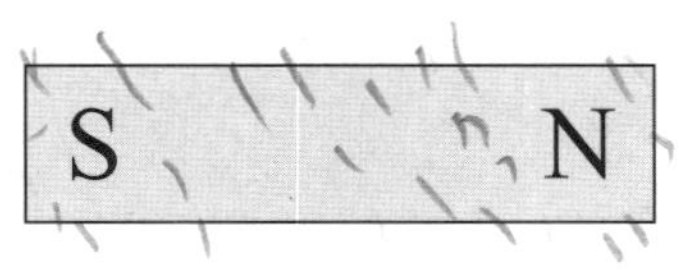

No look at answer booklet

(c) Briefly describe another way, apart from using iron filings, that Rhys can show the magnetic field around a bar magnet.

He could use any material that is magnetic. X

Place compass at various positions around magnet. It will always point from N to S along the field lines.

Magnets

1 Cassie is given four small metal bars. They all look the same, but her teacher says that one is copper, one is iron (but not a magnet) and the other two are magnets.

To find out which is which, Cassie holds the ends of two of the bars close to the ends of all the others, and records any **attraction** or **repulsion**, or whether the bars have **no effect** on each other. Her results are shown in the table below.

Bar	X	Y	Z
W	attraction	no effect	attraction
X		no effect	attraction and repulsion

(a) Which two bars are magnets? Explain how you know.

X and Z because they attract. X

(b) Which bar is made of iron, but is not a magnet? Explain how you know.

Z because it attracts and then repels. X

(c) Which bar is made of copper? Explain how you know.

Y because copper is non magnetic and therefore has NO effect

Cassie uses one bar magnet to push another one along the tabletop, then to pull it. Complete the diagrams below to show all the ways the poles could have lined up.

(d) One magnet pushing the other.

[S N] [S N] X or [N S] [N S] X

N S S N

(e) One magnet pulling the other.

[S N] [S N] or [N S] [N S]

Electromagnets

1 The circuit used for an alarm bell is shown below. It contains an electromagnet.

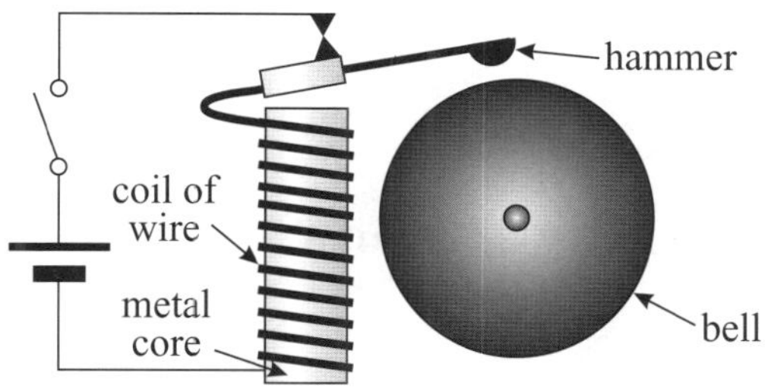

(a) (i) What name is given to the coil of wire in an electromagnet?

....

(ii) What metal is used to make the core of an electromagnet?

....

(b) The statements below describe how the circuit works, but they are in the wrong order. Write down their letters in the correct order.

A This completes the circuit again, and the cycle is repeated.
B When the switch is closed, the circuit is completed.
C Current stops flowing and the electromagnet is switched off.
D The electromagnet attracts the hammer.
E This happens several times a second, so the bell will ring continuously for as long as the switch is closed.
F The hammer moves, hitting the bell.
G The hammer is released and it returns to its original position.

1 .... 2 .... 3 .... 4 ....

5 .... 6 .... 7 ....

(c) Give **one** similarity between an electromagnet and a permanent bar magnet.

Same shape of magnetic field

(d) Give **two** differences between an electromagnet and a permanent bar magnet.

1 electromagnet switched on + off Permanent can't.

2 Electromagnets stronger than Permanet magnets.

Electromagnets

1 A simplified design for a switch-operated electric hand drier is shown below. The design contains two circuits, A and B.

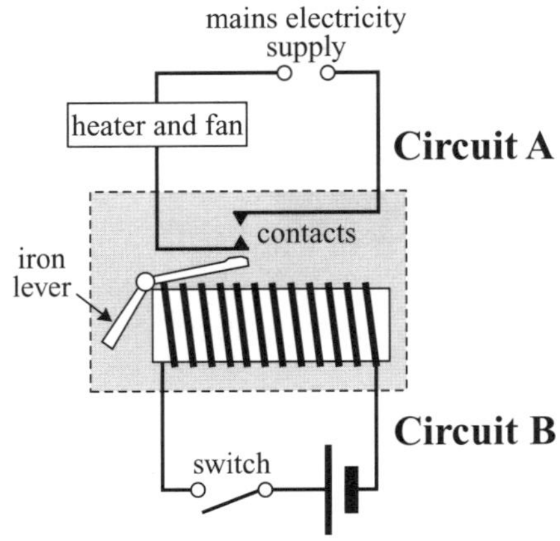

(a) Describe what happens when the switch in circuit **B** is closed.

....

....

....

(b) One of the circuits can be described as an input circuit and the other as an output circuit.

(i) Which is which?

Circuit .... **is an input circuit. Circuit** .... **is an output circuit.**

(ii) Explain your answer to (i).

....

....

(c) (i) What name is given to the part of the design in the shaded box?

....

(ii) This part of the design is used to prevent anyone using the drier from getting a bad electric shock from the mains electricity. Suggest how it does this.

....

....

Electricity and Magnetism Mini-Exam

1 In the circuit shown on the right,
the reading on ammeters $\mathbf{A_1}$ and $\mathbf{A_6}$ is 12 A.

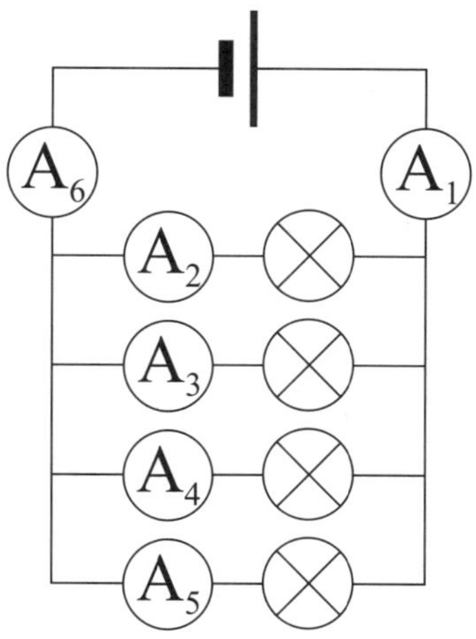

(a) (i) The bulbs in the circuit are identical.
What reading appears on **all** the ammeters $\mathbf{A_2}$ to $\mathbf{A_5}$?

....

(ii) Explain your answer to (i).

....

....

....

(b) Is any current used up in the circuit? What evidence is there for your answer?

....

....

2 Rajesh finds two metal bars on a shelf in the school laboratory.
Holding them near to each other, he notices a strong force of repulsion between the bars.
He decides that he has found two magnets.

(a) Is Rajesh correct? Explain your answer.

....

....

(b) In the diagram below, the north poles of two bar magnets are facing each other.
Draw in the field lines to show the shape of the magnetic fields around the poles.

Electricity and Magnetism Mini-Exam

3 Jess is having an operation to remove a small piece of metal from her eye. The surgeon uses a special instrument containing an electromagnet to remove it. Once the instrument is in the right position, he switches the electromagnet on and pulls the metal cleanly from Jess's eye.

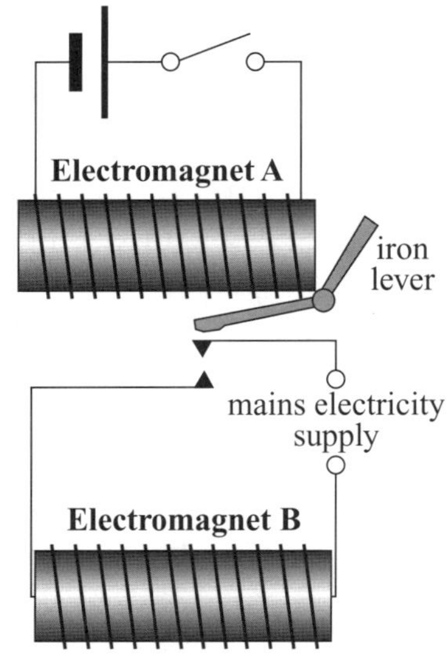

A simplified diagram of the instrument is shown on the right. As shown, it actually contains two electromagnets.

(a) Each electromagnet is made by winding a coil of insulated copper wire around an iron core.

(i) What name is given to the coil of wire used to make an electromagnet?

....

(ii) Why is copper a good material for making the electrical wire in the coil?

....

(iii) The wire is insulated to stop the current from jumping between turns in the coil. Suggest a material that would be suitable for insulating the wire.

....

(b) Electromagnet A is part of a **relay**. What is a **relay**?

....

(c) The sentences below describe how the instrument works.

A	**This pushes the contacts together,**	**turning on electromagnet B.**
B	**The lever is attracted to electromagnet A,**	**turning on electromagnet A.**
C	**The switch is closed by the surgeon,**	**and rotates towards it.**

(i) Draw lines to match the beginning of each sentence with the correct ending.

(ii) Write down the letters of the sentences in the correct order.

1 .... 2 .... 3 ....

Electricity and Magnetism Mini-Exam

(d) Complete the diagram below to show the field lines around electromagnet B when it is switched on.

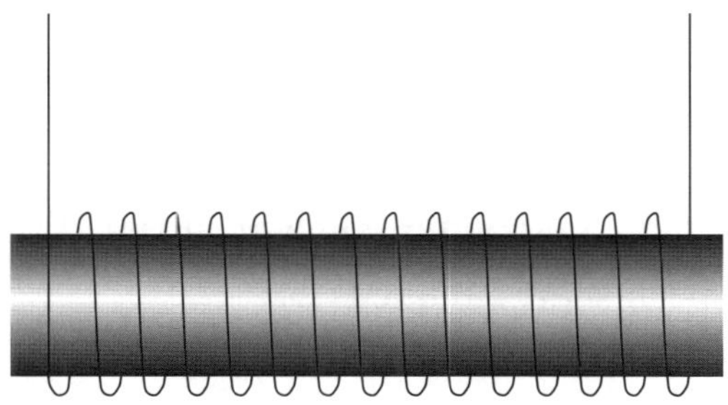

(e) (i) Which **two** of the following metals might have been stuck in Jess's eye? Underline your choices.

copper **steel** **tin** **aluminium** **lead** **nickel**

(ii) Explain your answer to (i).

....

....

(f) Suggest a reason why an electromagnet and not a permanent bar magnet is used to remove the metal from Jess's eye.

....

....

Electricity and Magnetism Mini-Exam

4 Brendan is installing two lights in his caravan, one for each room. The circuit he uses is shown in the diagram on the right.

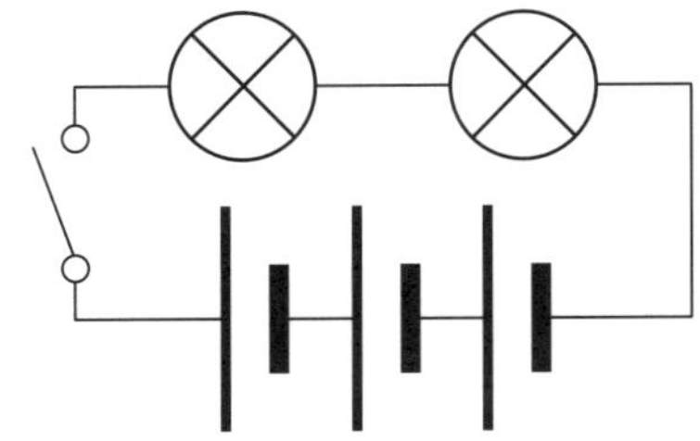

(a) Are the bulbs in Brendan's circuit connected in **series** or in **parallel**?

....

(b) When Brendan switches them on, both lights come on at first, then one goes out. Brendan decides that it has been short circuited.

(i) Explain what a **short circuit** is.

....

....

(ii) When the bulb goes out, what happens to the brightness of the other bulb in the circuit? Note that the bulbs Brendan is using are identical.

....

(iii) Explain your answer to (ii).

....

....

(c) Brendan wants to be able to switch the lights on and off one at a time.

(i) Explain why he can't do this using the circuit shown above.

....

....

(ii) Draw a circuit that will allow Brendan to control the lights separately. It should contain the battery and bulbs that Brendan is using, and **two** switches.

Speed

1 On the way home from school, Dervla timed how long she took to walk between two streetlights. She knows that the streetlights are 150 m apart.

(a) On Monday, she took 100 seconds to walk between the streetlights.
What speed was she walking at? Show your working and include the unit.

....

....

(b) On Tuesday, Dervla ran the distance between the two streetlights.
She calculates that her speed was 2 m/s. How much longer did it take her to walk between the streetlights on Monday than it took her to run on Tuesday, in seconds?
Show your working.

....

....

....

2 Clive cycles from his house up to the top of Beacon Hill.
He stops for a rest at the top, then turns around and freewheels down the hill back to his house. At the end of the ride, his cycle computer gives his **average** speed as 24 km/h.

(a) Why is the speed given by the computer an **average**?

....

....

(b) The whole ride takes three-quarters of an hour.
How far did Clive ride? Show your working and include the unit.

....

....

....

Speed

1 A train makes a non-stop journey of 540 km in 4 hours.

(a) What is the speed of the train in kilometres per hour?

....

(b) (i) How far does the train travel, in metres?

....

(ii) How long does the journey take, in seconds?

....

....

(iii) What is the speed of the train in metres per second?

....

....

2 Mark, Corin and Jodie are travelling by bike, car and on foot down the same stretch of road. Their speeds are shown below.

Name	**Speed**
Mark	36 km/h
Corin	2 kilometres per minute
Jodie	1.8 m/s

How far will each of them travel in one hour?

Mark ....

Corin ....

Jodie ....

Speed

1 A research scientist is investigating the properties of various liquids. He drops a metal ball down a tube filled with one of the liquids and measures the time taken for the ball to pass between two marks on the tube. The marks are 50 cm apart. Some of the results are shown in the table below.

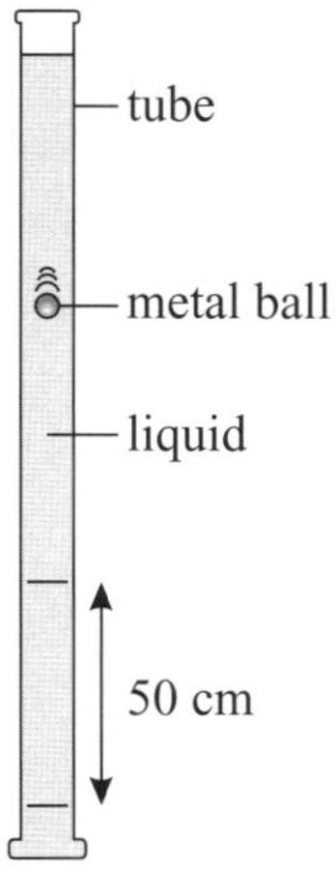

Liquid	Time taken to pass between marks	Speed
A	10 seconds	
B	2 seconds	
C	5 seconds	
D		1.0 m/s
E		2.5 m/s
F		0.4 m/s

(a) Did the ball drop more quickly through liquid A or through liquid B?

....

(b) What was the average speed of the ball between the marks in liquid C, in **metres per second**?

....

....

(c) How long did the ball take to pass between the marks in liquid D?

....

(d) How long would the ball take to pass through 15 m of liquid E?

....

(e) How far through liquid F would the ball travel in 23 seconds?

....

Force and Movement

1 A hot air balloon is floating along in mid-air. There are two forces acting on it — an upward force from the hot air inside the balloon and a downward force of gravity.

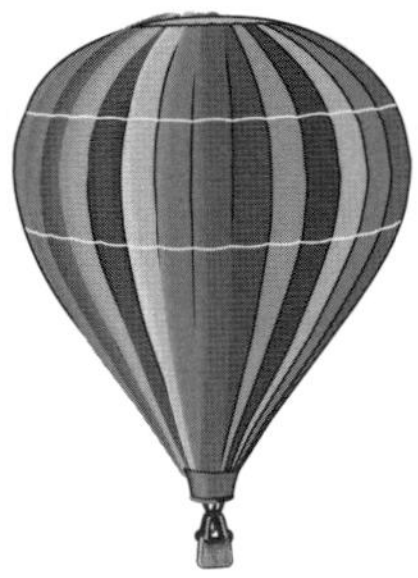

What will happen if

(a) The force from the hot air is larger than the force of gravity?

....

(b) The force of gravity is larger than the force from the hot air?

....

(c) The two forces are balanced?

....

2 The device shown opposite is used to measure forces. It contains a strong spring and a scale.

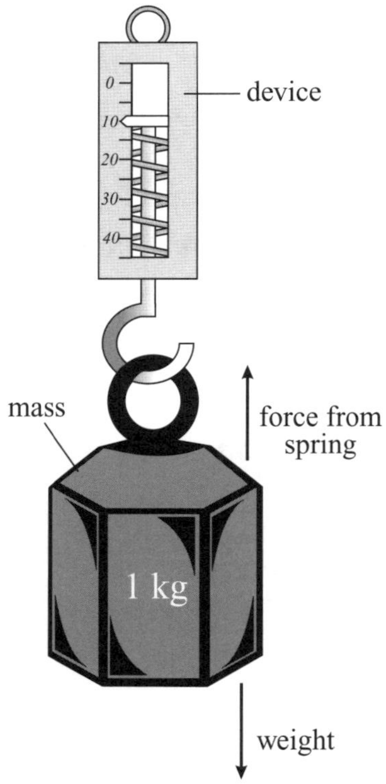

(a) (i) What is the name of the device?

....

(ii) What are the units on its scale?

....

A mass is shown hanging from the device. A pair of forces act on the mass, exerted by the spring and the weight of the mass.

(b) The pointer on the scale of the device is not moving. What can you say about

(i) the **sizes** of the two forces acting on the mass?

....

(ii) the **direction** of the two forces acting on the mass?

....

Force and Movement

1 In each of the diagrams below, forces are shown acting on objects.

A

An athlete pushes on the **wheels** of his wheelchair.

B

A **car** collides with a wall.

C

A **car** travels through a town at a steady speed of 30 miles per hour.

D

A tennis player hits the **ball** back to her opponent.

E

A **sprinter** pushes out of the blocks at the start of a race.

F

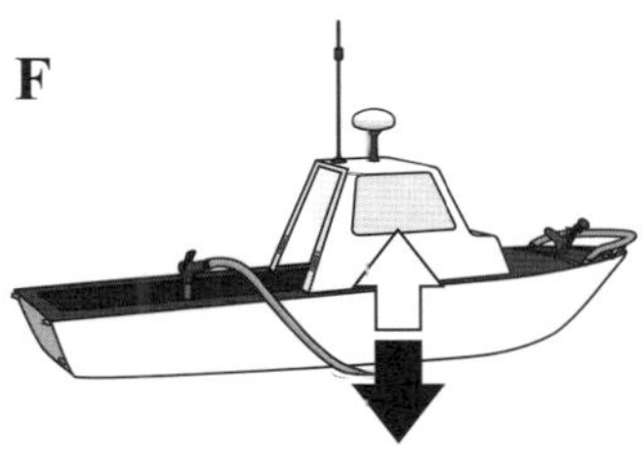

A **boat** floats on the water.

G

A parachute opens behind a fast-moving **dragster**.

(a) (i) In which **two** situations are forces balanced? .... **and** ....

(ii) Even though forces are balanced in both situations, the movement is different. What is the difference in movement between these two situations?

....

....

(b) Each of the **other** five situations shows a **different** effect of forces on movement. Write down the letter of the situation which **best** shows an object which is

(i) speeding up. ....

(ii) slowing down. ....

(iii) changing direction. ....

(iv) changing shape. ....

(v) turning. ....

(Each letter must be used once.)

Air Resistance and Friction

1 Hester is taking part in a javelin throwing competition.

To make a throw, she grips the javelin and runs towards the line.
She throws the javelin when she is still several metres away from the line,
so that she has room to stop before she gets to the line.
The javelin is accelerating as it flies out of Hester's hand,
then slows down gradually and lands about sixty metres away.

(a) Give **two** ways that frictional forces are helpful to Hester when throwing the javelin.

1 ....

2 ....

The diagram below shows the forces that act on the javelin during its flight.

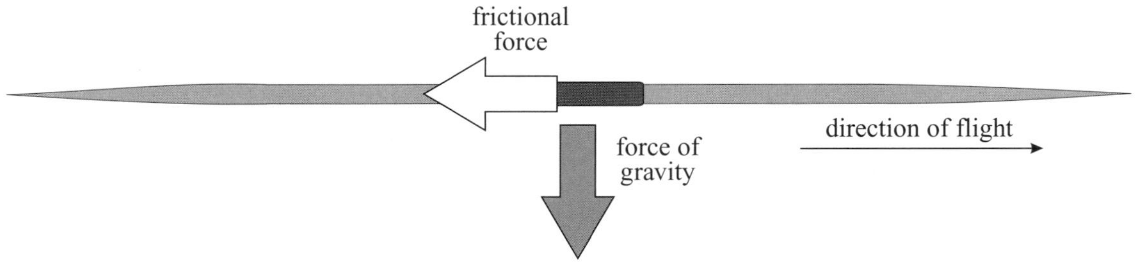

(b) The frictional force slows the javelin down.

(i) What term is used to describe this frictional force?

....

(ii) What will happen to the **size** of the frictional force as the javelin slows down?

....

(iii) What can you say about the **direction** of the frictional force acting on the javelin?

....

(c) Suggest what would happen if there was **no** frictional force acting on the javelin during its flight.

....

Air Resistance and Friction

1 A skydiver falling through the air has two opposing forces acting on her, one upward due to air resistance and one downward due to gravity.

(a) At the instant the skydiver steps out of the plane, there is no air resistance acting on her. As she falls, air resistance gradually increases. Explain why.

....

....

(b) (i) What happens to the air resistance when the skydiver's parachute opens?

....

(ii) Explain why the skydiver falls at a steady speed with the parachute open.

....

(c) Write down the letters of the diagrams and labels below in the correct order in the table.

	Diagram	Label
1	Z	C
2		
3		
4		
5		

A Steady speed

B Losing speed

C Rapidly gaining speed

D Weight equal to reaction force from ground

E Gradually gaining speed

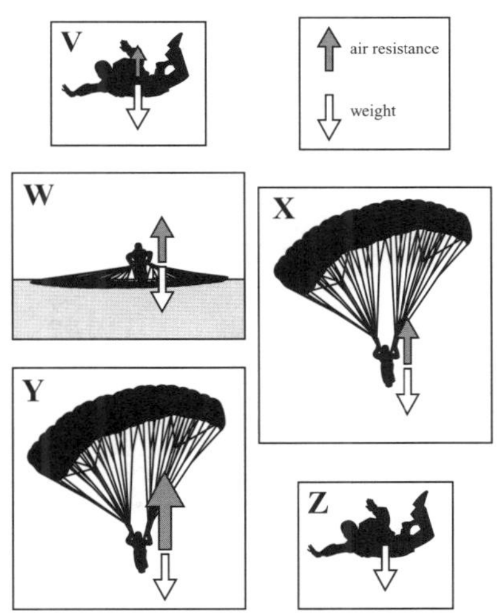

2 Two motorbikes, A and B, are identical apart from their shapes. The shape of motorbike B causes more air resistance.

(a) Which motorbike will have the higher top speed, A or B? ....

(b) If the motorbikes are travelling at the same speed, which one would you expect to use fuel more quickly? Explain your answer.

....

....

Force and Rotation

1 The diagram below shows Toby using a lever to raise a barrel of water.

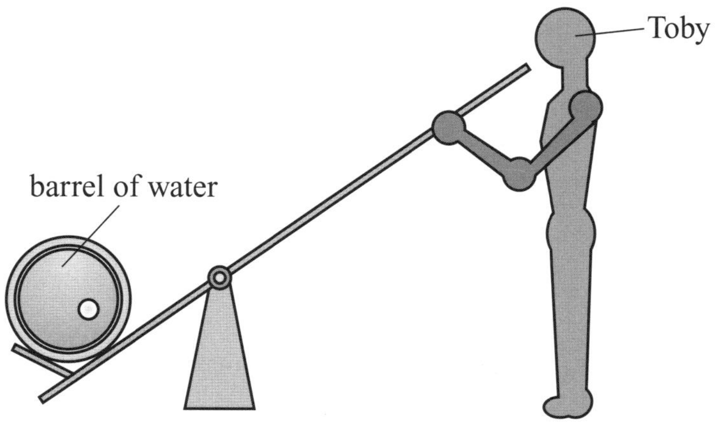

(a) (i) Add **two** arrows to the diagram to show the forces exerted by Toby and by the barrel. Label the arrows **effort force** and **load**.

(ii) Label the diagram to show where the **pivot** is.

(b) What is a pivot?

....

(c) Complete the following sentences by choosing words from the list below.

greater turning leverage smaller nearer direction distance size

The .... effect of a force depends on the

... of the force and its ....

from the point of rotation. The .... the distance between

the pivot and Toby's hands, the greater the .... ,

and the .... the effort force is compared to the load.

Force and Rotation

1 Sonja is using the wheelbarrow below to move some bricks.

(a) Label the **pivot** on the diagram above.

(b) Sonja piles the bricks in the barrow. Draw and label an arrow to show how you would expect the **load** to act on the barrow.

(c) (i) Which is the best point for Sonja to apply an effort force to the wheelbarrow, X or Y? Draw and label an arrow to show the **effort force** acting at this point.

(ii) Explain your answer to (i).

....

....

2 A tool-making company has designed two different wirecutters, shown below.

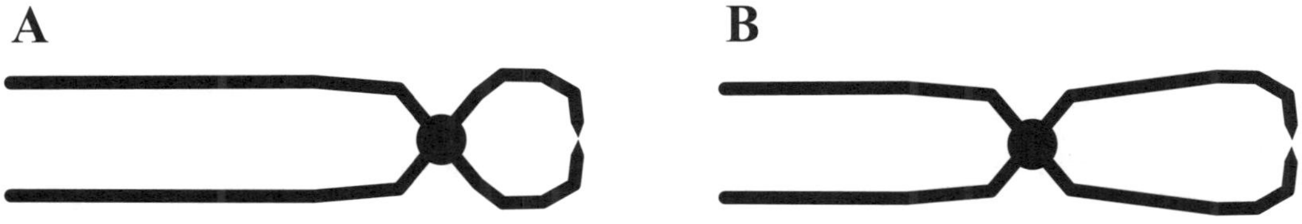

(a) Which design is better, A or B? ....

(b) Give **one** reason for your answer to (a).

....

....

Moments

1 At the playground, Josh sits on the roundabout while Ruth pushes it round.
The diagram shows the roundabout from above.

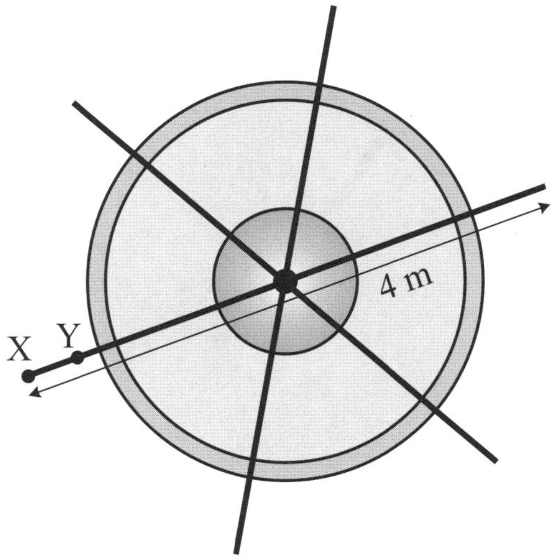

Ruth exerts a force at point X, which creates a **turning force** about the roundabout's pivot that makes it turn **anticlockwise**.

(a) On the diagram above

(i) Label the **pivot**.

(ii) Draw an arrow to show the force exerted by Ruth.

(b) (i) What name is given to a turning force?

....

(ii) How far from the pivot does Ruth push on the roundabout?

....

(iii) Ruth pushes with a force of 80 N. What turning force will act about the pivot? Show your working and give the units.

....

....

(c) Ruth moves her hands so that she pushes on the roundabout at point Y.
Is it easier or more difficult for her to push Josh round? Explain your answer.

....

....

Moments

1 The diagram below shows a set of scales used to measure rice.
Rice is placed in the dish, and the mass is moved along the arm until the scales balance.

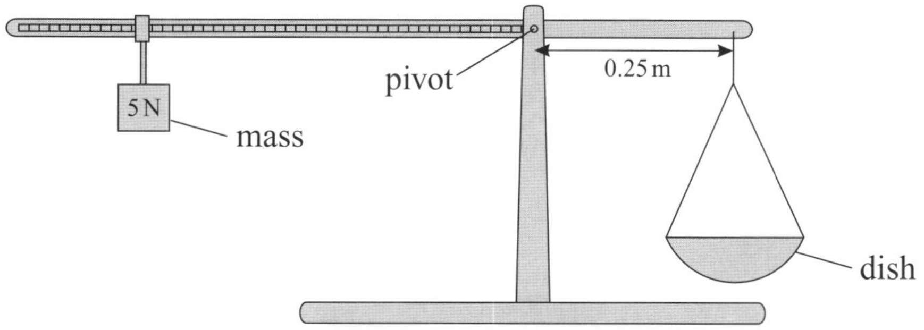

(a) The weight of the rice and the weight of the mass create moments about the pivot. What can you say about the directions of the moments created by the rice and the mass?

....

....

A bag of rice with weight 10 N is placed in the dish.

(b) What moment is caused by the rice? Show your working.

....

....

(c) The mass is placed 0.5 m from the pivot. Will the scales balance?
Show your working and explain your answer.

....

....

(d) For a different bag of rice, the scales balance when the mass is 0.1 m from the pivot.
What is the weight of the bag of rice? Show your working and give the unit.

....

....

....

Moments

1 The diagram below shows one instant during the swing of a pendulum. The pendulum is hung from the pivot point by a wire 50 cm long. The weight of the pendulum (10 N) creates a moment about the pivot.

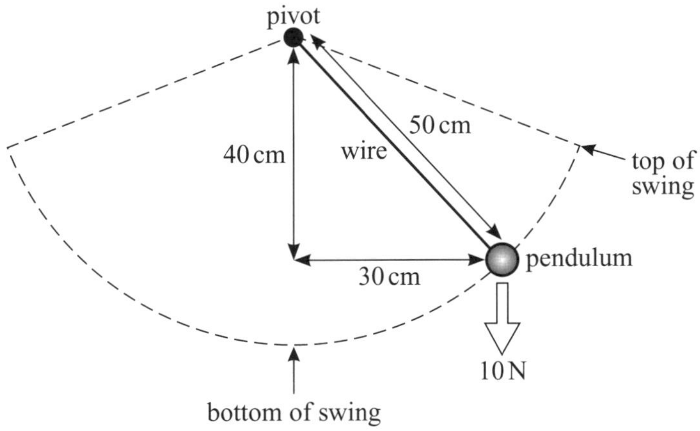

(a) The length of 30 cm in the diagram above can be used to calculate the moment created by the weight of the pendulum. Explain why.

....

....

(b) Calculate the moment of the pendulum about the pivot. Show your working and give the units.

....

(c) (i) What will happen to the moment you calculated in (b) as the pendulum moves towards the top of its swing?

....

(ii) What will happen to the moment you calculated in (b) as the pendulum moves towards the bottom of its swing?

....

(iii) Explain your answers to (i) and (ii).

....

....

....

Pressure

1 Mairi is pushing a drawing pin into a wall with a force of 20 N.

(a) She pushes on the flat head of the drawing pin, which has an area of 0.8 cm^2.
What is the pressure on the head of the drawing pin, **in N/cm^2**? Show your working.

....

(b) The point of the drawing pin is blunt, and has an area of 0.01 cm^2.
What is the pressure on the point of the drawing pin, in N/cm^2? Show your working.

....

(c) Instead of going into the wall, the pin bends. Mairi takes another, sharper pin and pushes it with the same force as before. Explain why this pin enters the wall easily.

....

....

....

2 Anne has bought a statue for her garden, but the ground where she wants to put it is soft. If the pressure of the statue on the ground goes over 4000 Pa, it will sink.

(a) The statue weighs 450 N and has an area of contact with the ground of 0.06 m^2. Anne thinks it will sink.
Is she correct? Show your working.

....

....

(b) She decides to make a base for the statue out of concrete.
Explain how adding a base can reduce the pressure of the statue on the ground.

....

....

....

Pressure

1 The pond in Max's back garden has iced over. Max wants to see if it is safe to walk on. He stands with both feet on the ice, and finds that it does not crack. He says "the ice holds my weight, so it is safe to walk on."

(a) Each foot exerts a pressure of 12 000 Pa on the ice, and the area of contact between the soles of Max's feet and the ice is 0.06 m^2. Use the formula $F = P \times A$ to calculate Max's weight. Show your working and give the units.

....

(b) What will the pressure on the ice be if Max stands on one foot? Explain your answer.

....

....

(c) Max's finding that the ice will hold his **weight** is correct. Explain why his conclusion that the ice is safe to walk on may not be correct.

....

....

2 A company is designing an alarm button that an elderly person can carry with them and use if they need to call for help. The alarm is set off when the plate is pressed hard enough to create a pressure of 4 N/cm^2.

(a) In the first design of the button, the plate has an area of 9 cm^2. What force is needed to set off the alarm?

....

....

(b) The designers want to reduce the force needed to set off the alarm to 28 N. Use the formula $A = F / P$ to calculate the area the plate should be.

....

....

Pressure

1 Alan is building a house. He knows that, for safety, the pressure on the soil should not be more than 29 000 Pa. He has enough space to build foundations of area 7.25 m^2.

(a) Use the formula F = P × A to calculate the maximum weight that Alan can build on this area. Show your working and include the units.

....

....

(b) Alan builds the maximum area of foundations and finds that they weigh 58 000 N. What is the maximum weight of the house that Alan can build on these foundations?

....

....

2 Isobel is driving her truck off-road. She decides to let some air out of the truck's tyres before crossing some soft, marshy ground.

(a) Explain how letting the tyres down could help Isobel get her truck across the marsh.

....

....

The truck weighs 24 000 N. If it exerts pressure of more than 40 000 Pa on the marshy ground, it will sink. Before being let down, the tyres make 0.4 m^2 of contact with the ground.

(b) Use the formula A = F / P to calculate how much **bigger** the tyres' area of contact with the ground must be for the truck to cross the marsh without sinking.

....

....

....

Forces and Motion Mini-Exam

1 The diagram below shows forces that affect the movement of a cyclist.

(a) Drag is a frictional force that acts against the cyclist's movement.

(i) What causes drag?

....

(ii) Give **one** way that frictional forces (other than drag) are useful to the cyclist.

....

The cyclist takes 12.5 s to travel 160 m.
During this time, he produces enough forward force to equal the drag acting on him.

(b) Does the cyclist's speed change during this time? Explain your answer.

....

....

(c) What is the cyclist's speed? Show your working and give the units.

....

The cyclist increases the forward force he is producing.

(d) Cross out **six** words so that the sentences below are correct.

The forward force is smaller / bigger than the drag, so the forces acting on the cyclist are unbalanced / balanced and his speed decreases / increases.
The drag then decreases / increases until the forces acting on him are unbalanced / balanced and he reaches a new, lower / higher constant speed.

(e) The cyclist's new speed is 14.8 m/s. How long will he take to travel 160 m at this speed? Show your working.

....

Forces and Motion Mini-Exam

2 Joseph is arranging a set of four books on his new bookshelf.
Each book has the dimensions shown opposite and weighs 27 N.

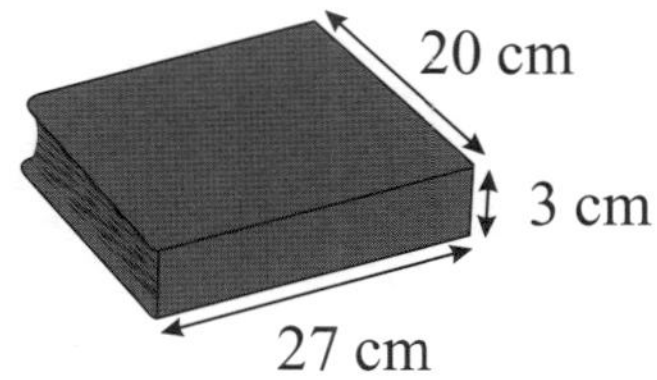

First, he tries the arrangement shown in A below,
then he tries the arrangement shown in B.

(a) How much pressure will arrangement A put on the bookshelf, **in N/cm²**?
Show your working.

....

....

(b) How much **less** pressure will arrangement B put on the bookshelf, in **N/cm²**?
Show your working.

....

....

....

(c) Joseph decides to use arrangement B.
The weight of the books creates a moment about
point P where the shelf is fixed to the wall, as shown.
A moment greater than 20 Nm will cause the shelf to fall down.

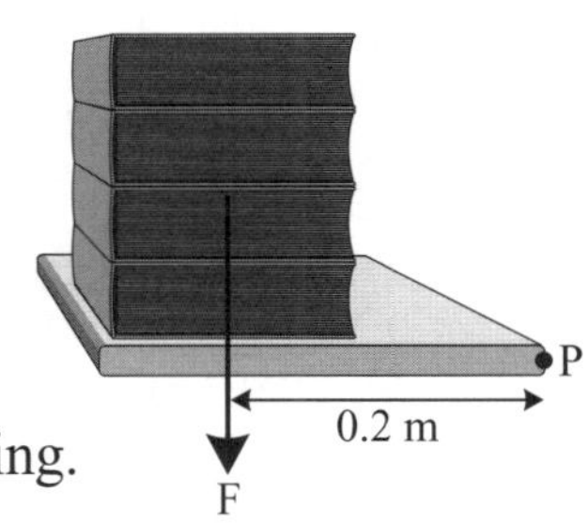

(i) Will the books cause the shelf to fall down? Show your working.

....

(ii) What could John do to reduce the moment about point P? Explain your answer.

....

....

Forces and Motion Mini-Exam

3 A door is fitted with a closing device to stop the wind blowing it open. In diagram B below, force W is the force of the wind against the door, and force C is the force exerted by the closing device.

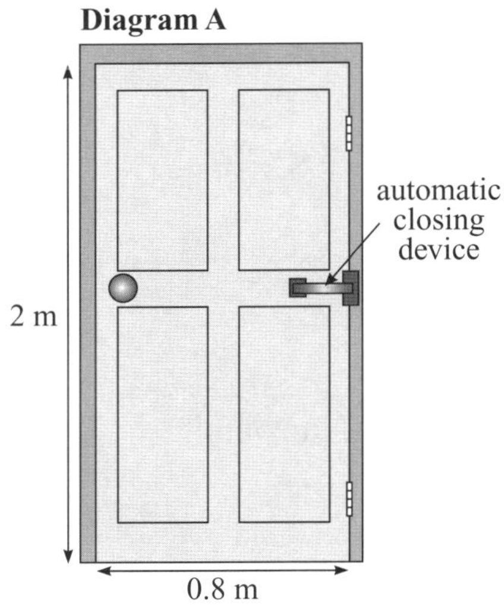

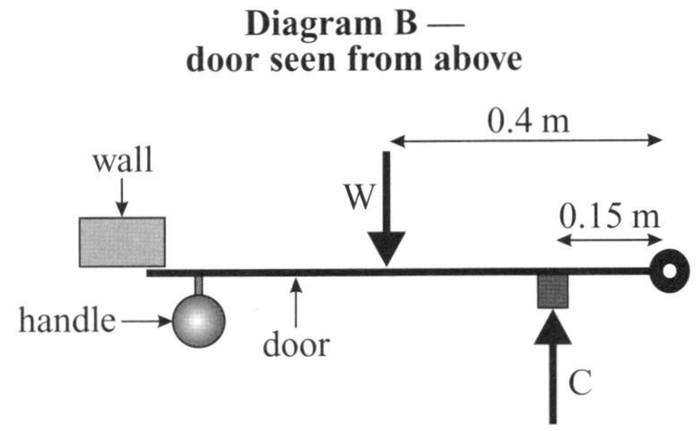

(a) The door acts as a lever.

(i) Label the **pivot** on **diagram B**.

(ii) Which of the two forces is the **effort force** and which is the **load**?

Force W is the ....

Force C is the ....

(b) The wind blowing onto the door exerts a pressure on it of 20 Pa.

(i) Use diagram A to work out the area the wind exerts this pressure on, in m^2. Show your working.

....

(ii) What is the force of the wind on the door, in newtons? Show your working.

....

(c) (i) As shown in diagram B, the force of the wind acts at a perpendicular distance of 0.4 m from the pivot. Calculate the moment of the force about the pivot. Show your working and give the unit.

....

Forces and Motion Mini-Exam

(ii) The moment produced by the closing device about the pivot is 10 Nm.
Will the door be blown open by the wind? Explain your answer.

....

....

....

The wind stops. In the diagram below, force C is the force exerted by the closing device and force J is the force exerted by Jessica pulling on the door handle.

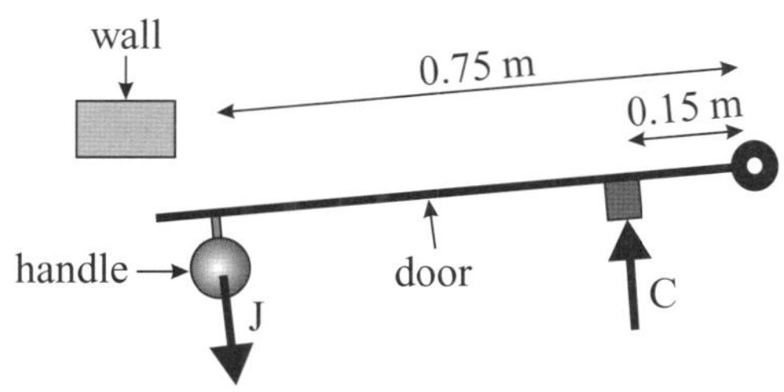

(d) Force C is 40 N. What is the moment of force C about the pivot?
Show your working.

....

(e) (i) Jessica is holding the door so that it stays in the position shown above.
What is the moment of force J about the pivot?

....

(ii) Calculate the value of force J, in newtons.

....

(f) Explain why Jessica can hold the door open with a force that is smaller than force C.

....

....

(g) What will happen to the movement of the door if force C stays the same and force J

(i) **increases?** ....

(ii) **decreases?** ....

Properties of Light

1 Meera uses the pinhole camera in the diagram below to trace an image of a tree.

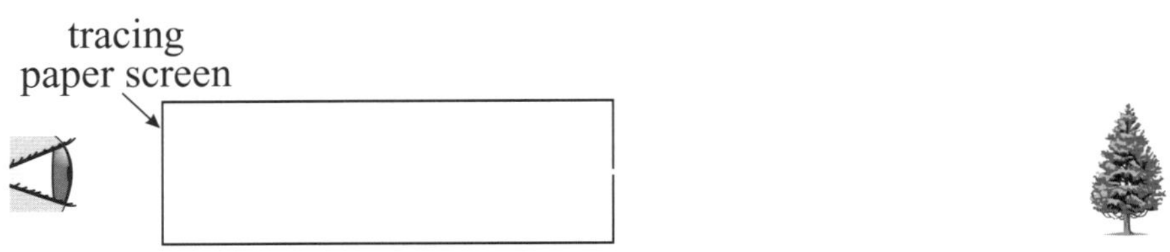

When she compares the tree on the tracing paper screen with the real tree, the two images are different.

(a) How is the image on the screen different from the image of the real tree? Tick the correct box.

- [ ] **Upside down, back-to-front and black and white.**
- [ ] **The right way up but back-to-front.**
- [ ] **Back-to-front and upside down.**
- [ ] **Upside down but the right way round.**
- [ ] **The right way round but upside down and brighter.**

(b) Draw lines on the diagram at the top to show how the image of the tree is formed on the tracing paper screen.

(c) What property of light explains why the image of the tree on the screen is different from the image of the real tree? Tick the correct box.

- [ ] **Light will not travel through an opaque object.**
- [ ] **Light travels very quickly.**
- [ ] **Light travels in straight lines.**
- [ ] **Light always travels at the same speed through air.**

Properties of Light

1 Charmaine enters a darkened room, and switches on a table lamp.
There is a mug on the table in front of her.

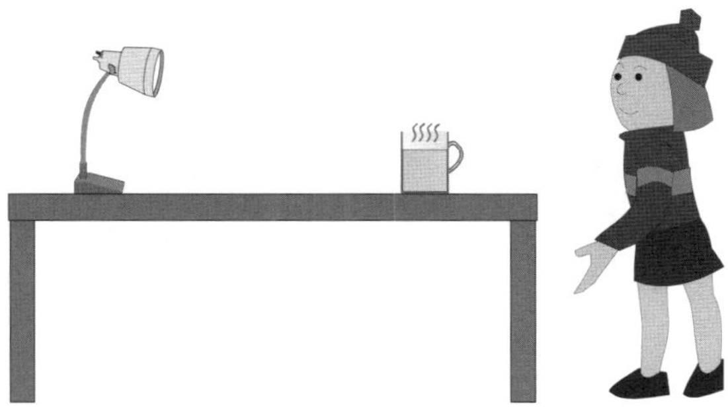

(a) Use the words in the list below to fill in the gaps in the sentences that follow.

travels directly **non-luminous** **luminous** **is reflected**

Charmaine is able to see the light bulb because it is a

.. object.

Light .... from the bulb to Charmaine's eye.

The mug is a .... object.

She can see it because light .... from it to her eye.

(b) Draw rays of light on the diagram above to show how Charmaine is able to see

(i) the light bulb. (ii) the mug.

2 Arif is watching a firework display at his local park.

(a) Explain why Arif can see the fireworks explode even though it is dark.

....

(b) Why does Arif hear the explosions only **after** he has seen them?

....

Reflection

1 The diagram below shows a ray of light hitting a mirror.

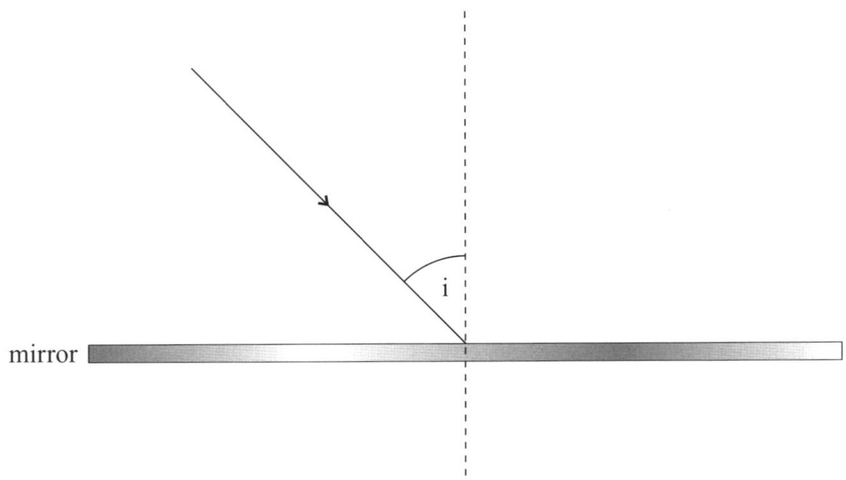

(a) What happens to a ray of light when it hits a mirror?

....

(b) Add the following two labels to the diagram.

normal **incident ray**

(c) (i) What is the angle, **i**, shown in the diagram above?

Angle i is the angle of ....

(ii) Draw the **reflected light ray** and the **angle of reflection**, **r** on the diagram.

(d) (i) What is the relationship between the size of the angles **i** and **r**?

....

(ii) Which property of a mirror causes this relationship between the size of the angles **i** and **r**?

....

....

Reflection

1 The **law of reflection** states that the angle of reflection is equal to the angle of incidence. The diagram below shows rays of light from a candle being reflected from a curved mirror. The reflected image on the screen is upside down and sharply focused.

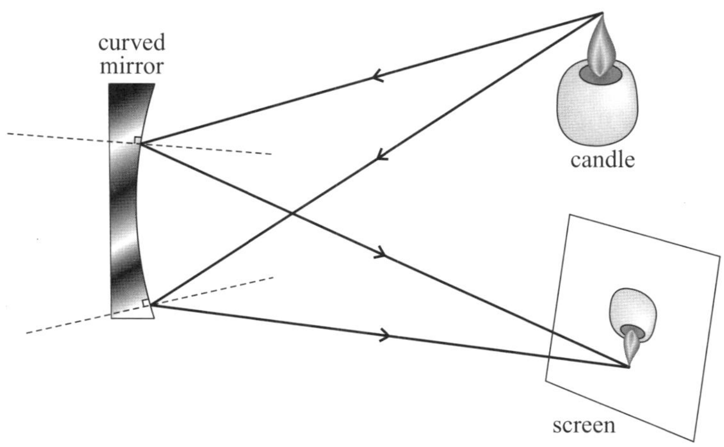

(a) Does the light falling on the mirror in the diagram above obey the law of reflection?

....

(b) The curved mirror brings the rays of light from the candle together so that the image on the screen is in sharp focus. Would the mirror reflect a sharp image onto the screen if it was not curved? Explain your answer.

....

(c) Predict what will happen to the **size** of the image on the screen if the candle is brought closer to the mirror.

....

(d) (i) Do rays of light falling on a sheet of paper obey the law of reflection? Explain your answer.

....

(ii) What term is used to describe the type of reflection that happens when light falls on a sheet of paper?

....

(iii) What effect does this have on the appearance of the paper? Tick the correct box.

☐ **It looks rough.** ☐ **It looks shiny.** ☐ **It looks dull.**

Refraction

1 Light can be bent when it passes from one medium to another.

(a) (i) All the media that light can pass between have one property in common. What is it? Tick the correct box.

☐ **They have a high density.** ☐ **They are opaque.**

☐ **They are transparent.** ☐ **They have a low density.**

(ii) What name is given to the bending of light as it passes between media?

....

(b) (i) Use the words below to complete the sentences that follow.

a right angle **away from** **an angle** **towards**

When a light ray passes from air into glass it will bend

.. the normal if it is at

.. to the glass. When the ray passes from the

glass back into air it will bend .... the normal.

The light ray will not bend if it enters the glass at

.. to the glass.

(ii) Complete the diagrams below to show the path taken by a ray of light as it passes from air into the glass blocks and back into air.

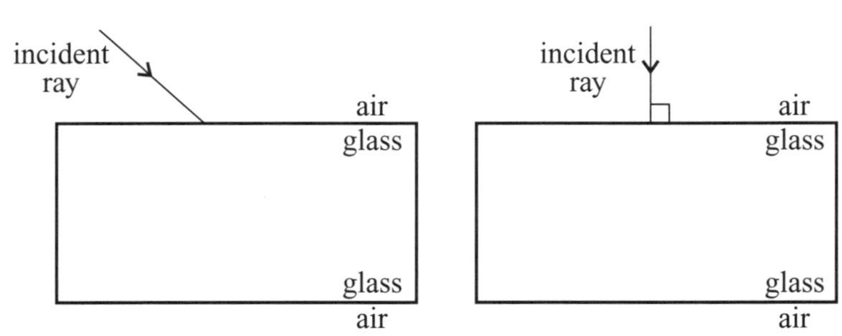

Refraction

1 Light bends when it passes between media because they have different densities.

(a) What property of light is affected by the density of the medium it is travelling in?

....

Lesley is investigating the density of various materials, and the effect of this on how much light bends. She sets up two experiments. In the first one, she shines a ray of light so that it travels from air into water. In the second one, the ray travels from air into glass. Her results are shown below.

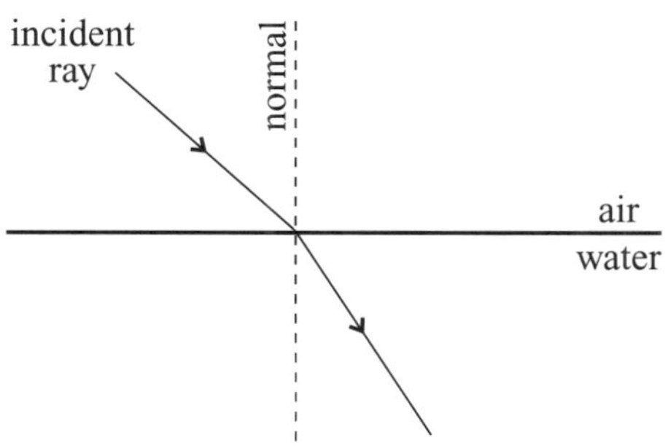

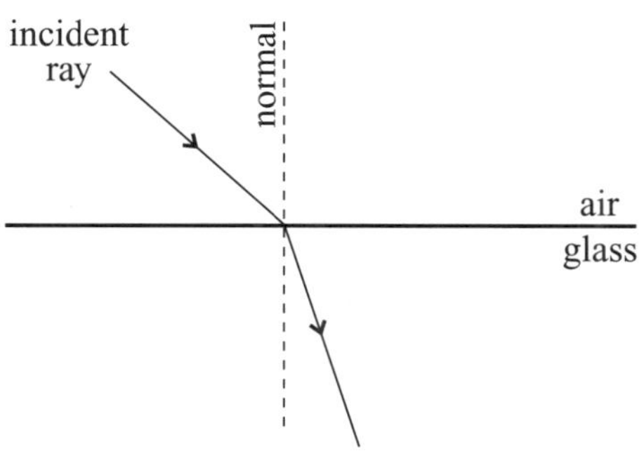

(b) Lesley knows that "the higher the density of the medium, the more light slows down when it enters." From her results, which medium would you expect to have the higher density, **water** or **glass**? Explain your answer.

....

....

....

(c) Complete the diagram below to show how you would expect light to bend as it travels from **water** to **glass**.

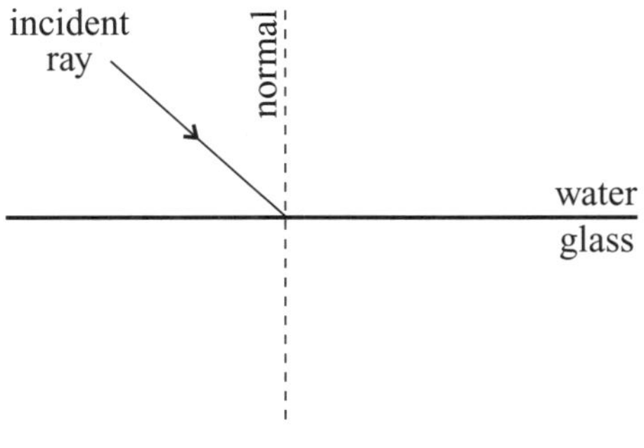

Colour

1 When white light shines on a glass prism it bends and is split up into different colours. In the diagram below, a rainbow pattern appears on the screen.

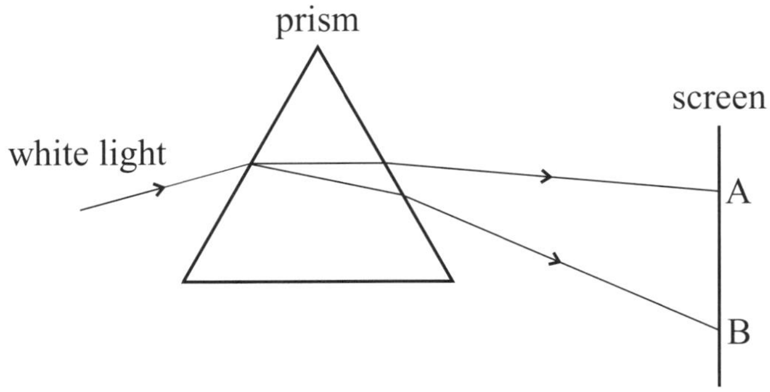

(a) Fill in the missing words to complete the sentence below.

When white light is split up or .... by a prism the

rainbow pattern that forms is called a ....

(b) (i) Name the colour that appears at **A** on the screen.

....

(ii) Name the colour that appears at **B** on the screen.

....

(iii) Why do the different colours spread out when white light shines on a prism?

....

....

(c) A rainbow is a natural example of light being split into different colours.

(i) What is the source of the white light that is split up when a rainbow forms?

....

(ii) What splits up the different colours when a rainbow forms?

....

Colour

1 Josie and Emma are using the school darkroom to develop some photographs. When they are ready to start, Emma switches off the lights and switches on a lamp that gives out only red light. She notices that Josie's clothes appear to change colour.

(a) Explain why, in the normal white light of the darkroom,

(i) Josie's T-shirt looks red.

....

(ii) Josie's jeans look blue.

....

(iii) Josie's trainers look white.

....

(b) What colour will Josie's clothes appear to be in the red light from the lamp? Explain your answers.

(i) **Her T-shirt will look** .... **because** ....

....

(ii) **Her jeans will look** .... **because** ....

....

(iii) **Her trainers will look** .... **because** ....

....

(c) Emma finds some filters on a shelf.

(i) With the red lamp still on, she looks at Josie through a red filter. What colour will her T-shirt appear to be? Explain your answer.

....

(ii) She puts a blue filter between the red filter and her eyes. What colour will Josie's T-shirt appear to be now? Explain your answer.

....

....

Light and Sound Mini-Exam — Part One

1 A light bulb is made up of a metal filament, enclosed in a glass bulb filled with a gas. Terry screws a new bulb into a lamp and switches it on. The filament glows brightly.

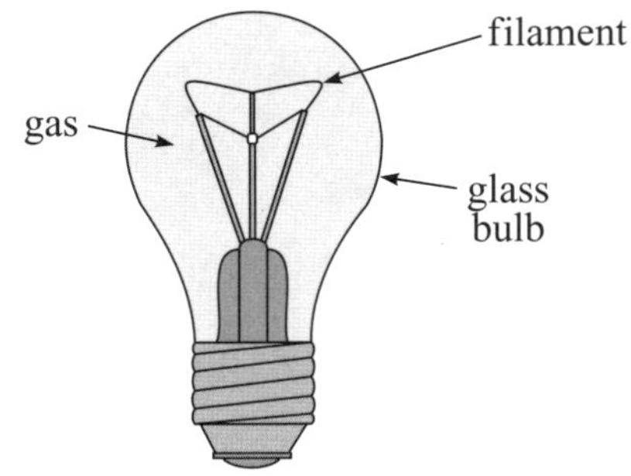

(a) (i) What term can be used to describe the filament when the lamp is switched on? Tick the correct box.

☐ **opaque** ☐ **transparent** ☐ **luminous** ☐ **reflective**

(ii) Terry is able to see the light bulb both before and after he switches it on, but the **way** he is able to see it changes. Describe how it changes.

....

....

(b) The light given out by the filament is refracted when it passes from the gas in the bulb into the glass, and again when it passes from the glass into the air in the room.

(i) What does **refracted** mean, in terms of light?

....

(ii) What can you say about the density of the gas in the bulb compared to the density of the glass?

....

(iii) Complete the diagram below to show what happens to one ray of the light from the filament as it passes from the **glass** of the bulb into **air**.

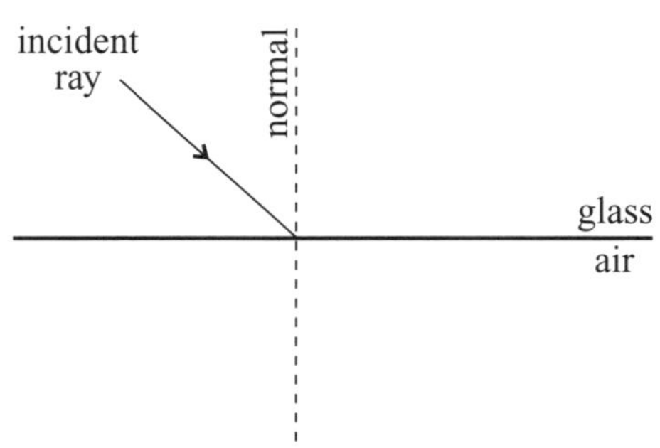

Light and Sound Mini-Exam — Part One

Terry uses a prism to disperse the light from the bulb. He gets the spectrum shown below.

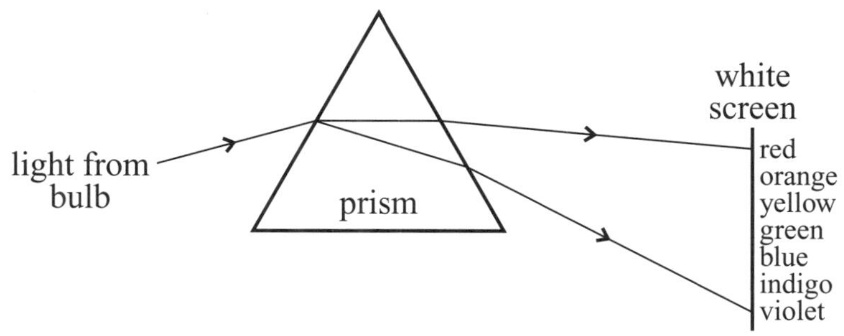

(c) What happens when light is **dispersed**?

....

(d) What colour is the light from the bulb? Explain your answer.

....

....

Terry places a red filter between the bulb and the prism.

(e) (i) Will the light from the bulb still be dispersed? Explain your answer.

....

....

(ii) What will Terry now see on the screen?

....

(f) Terry leaves the red filter in place, but replaces the white screen with a blue one.
He can no longer see anything on the screen. Explain why not.

....

....

Light and Sound Mini-Exam — Part One

2 Sharon has a picture frame made from wood and glass on her desk.

(a) Use the list of properties below to answer the questions that follow.

A	rough	**D**	non-luminous
B	luminous	**E**	transparent
C	opaque	**F**	smooth

(i) Which property of the glass explains why Sharon is able to see the photograph behind it? Write down the correct letter.

....

(ii) Which property of the glass explains why Sharon is also able to see her own reflection in it? Write down the correct letter.

....

(iii) Which property of the wood in the frame explains why it looks dull? Write down the correct letter.

....

(b) The diagram shows a ray of light shining onto the glass of the frame.

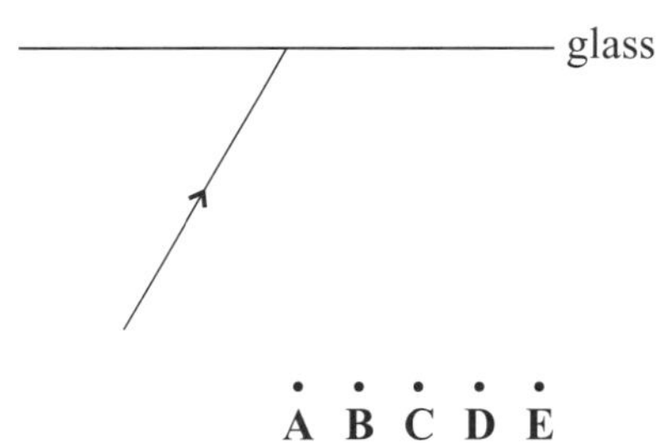

(i) The ray that is reflected from the glass is called the **reflected ray**. What term is used to describe the ray falling on the glass?

....

(ii) Which of the points **A** to **E** on the diagram will the reflected ray pass through? Explain how you know.

....

....

(iii) Explain why it would not be possible to answer (i) if the diagram showed a ray of light falling on the **wood** in the frame.

....

Sound

1 Joel is standing on top of a hill when a low-flying jet passes below him. It is flying faster than the speed of sound, and Joel sees the jet before he hears it.

(a) Why is Joel able to see the jet before he can hear it?

....

(b) At the same time as the sound of the jet reaches him, Joel feels the ground under his feet shake a little. Explain how the sound of the jet makes this happen.

....

(c) Use the words in the list below to complete the following sentence about sound.

vibration **waves** **energy** **a medium**

Sound is a form of .... **, carried through**

.... **by** .... **of**

.... **.**

2 Yasmin stands at the mouth of a cave and claps her hands. She hears the sound twice, first at the time she claps her hands and then again a few moments later.

(a) (i) What happens to the sound that means Yasmin hears it twice?

....

(ii) What is this called?

....

(b) Yasmin knows that sound travels at a speed of about 300 m/s in air. Suggest how she could use this information to estimate the size of the cave.

....

....

Sound

1 Ivan is using an oscilloscope connected to a microphone to investigate sounds.
He plays three notes on his violin, and obtains traces of the sound waves he makes.
The traces are shown below. They all have the same amplitude.

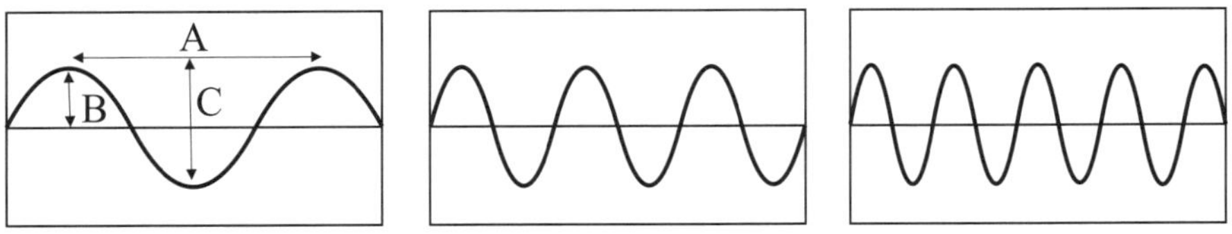

G sharp C natural E flat

(a) Which line represents amplitude, **A**, **B** or **C**? ....

(b) All three notes have a different pitch. In what way do they sound the same?

....

(c) Ivan plays another note, and this time the trace has a smaller amplitude.
Describe **two** things Ivan might have done that would make the amplitude smaller.

1 ....

2 ....

2 Oscilloscope traces were obtained for the following sounds.
The same oscilloscope settings were used for each one.

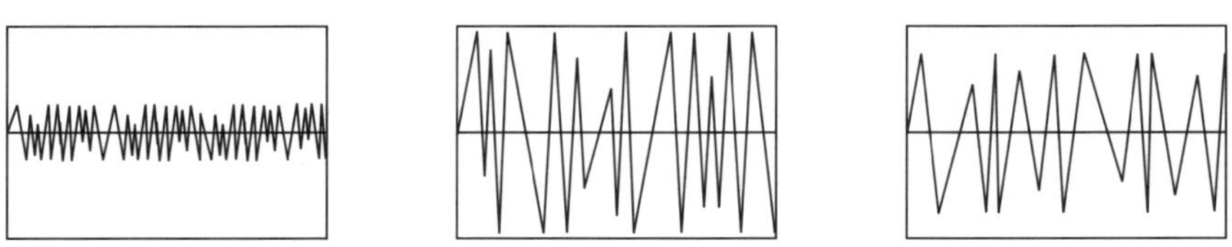

A — quiet talking **B** — a rock band **C** — road traffic

(a) Which of the sounds

(i) was quietest, **A**, **B** or **C**? ....

(ii) had the most energy, **A**, **B** or **C**? ....

(b) On the oscilloscope screen below, draw how you would expect the trace for the sound of a whisper to look.

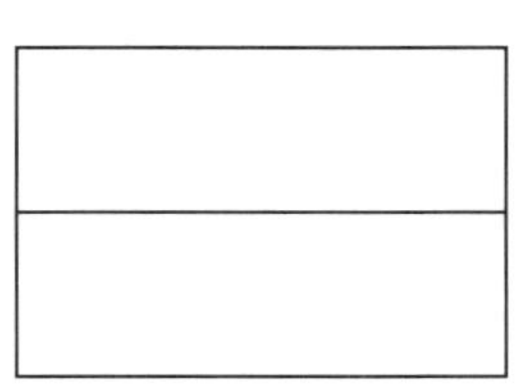

Sound

1 The oscilloscope traces for four different noises are shown below.

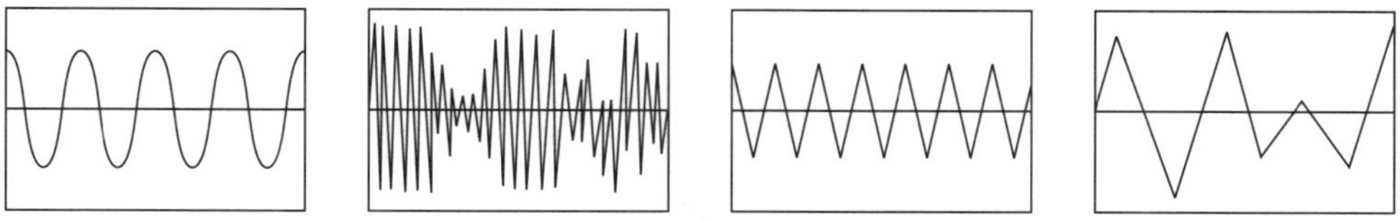

a car engine | a scream | a dentist's drill | a road drill

(a) Complete the definition of **frequency** by filling in the missing words in the sentence below.

Frequency is the number of .... sound waves

that pass a point in ....

(b) Write the sounds shown in the diagram above in order of frequency, lowest first.

1 .... 2 ....

3 .... 4 ....

(c) As the frequency of the vibration causing a noise increases, what will happen to the way the noise sounds?

....

2 The siren of a police car makes four different sounds. Oscilloscope traces for the sounds are shown below.

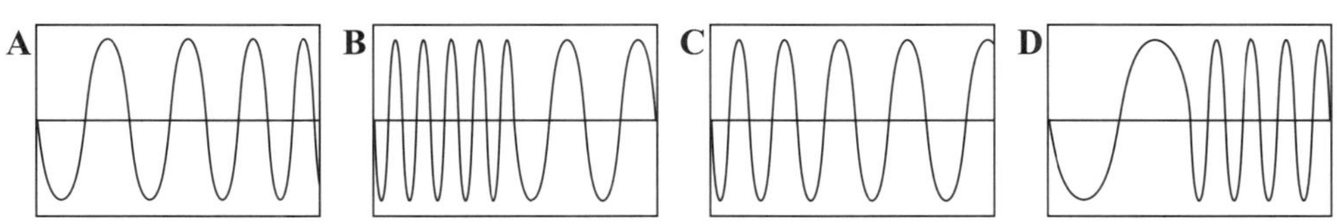

Answer the questions below by writing down the correct letters.

(a) Which two sounds start lower and get higher-pitched? .... **and** ....

(b) The pitch changes gradually for which two sounds? .... **and** ....

(c) Which two sounds contain two separate notes? .... **and** ....

Hearing

1 Julie whispers to Heather during a lesson.

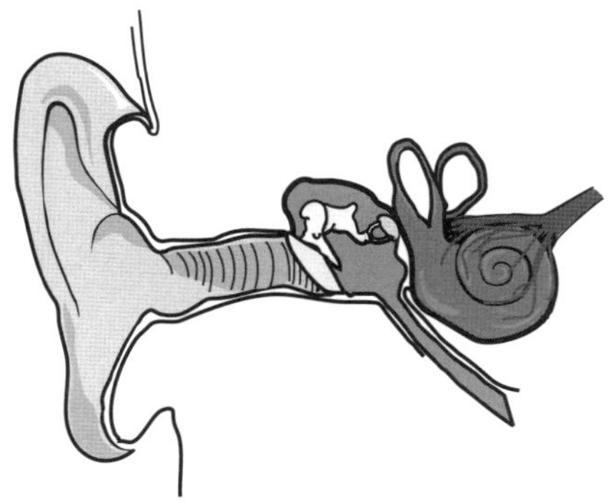

(a) Label the following parts of Heather's ear on the diagram above.

semi-circular canals **ear drum** **cochlea**
ear bones **Eustachian tube** **auditory nerve**

(b) When Julie whispers, the vocal cords in her throat vibrate.
Use the diagram to help you describe what happens to these vibrations so that Heather hears them as the sound of Julie's whisper.

....

....

....

....

(c) The table opposite shows the loudness of some sounds.

Sound	Loudness (dB)
Quietest sound it is possible to hear	1
Quiet talking	40
A busy classroom	70

(i) What does dB stand for?

....

(ii) Use the table to estimate the loudness of Julie's whisper.

....

(iii) The teacher is standing next to Julie.
Suggest why Heather hears Julie's whisper but the teacher does not.

....

....

Hearing

1 People in different jobs are exposed to different levels of noise.

(a) Draw lines to match each person to the noise level they are most likely to experience.

aeroplane engineer	60 dB
teacher	110 dB
traffic warden	80 dB
rock musician	130 dB

(b) Which people in the list above are risking damage to their hearing?

....

2 The table below shows the **approximate** audible range of frequencies that can be heard by five different animals. The names of the animals have been left out.

Animal	Audible range (Hz)
	125 – 2000
	2000 – 110 000
	75 – 150 000
	90 – 22 800
	16 – 120 000

(a) Use the information below to complete the table with the names in bold.

A **chinchilla**'s audible range is similar to a human's.
The **chicken** has the smallest audible range of the five animals.
The **porpoise** has the largest audible range of the five animals.
The **elephant** can hear sounds of a lower frequency than any of the others.
The **bat** is the only animal in the table that cannot hear a sound of 150 Hz.

(b) What does Hz stand for? ....

(c) Give **two** possible reasons why the ranges shown in the table are not exact.

1 ....

2 ....

Light and Sound Mini-Exam — Part Two

1 Tom's new clock has four different alarm sounds.
The oscilloscope trace for each sound is shown below.

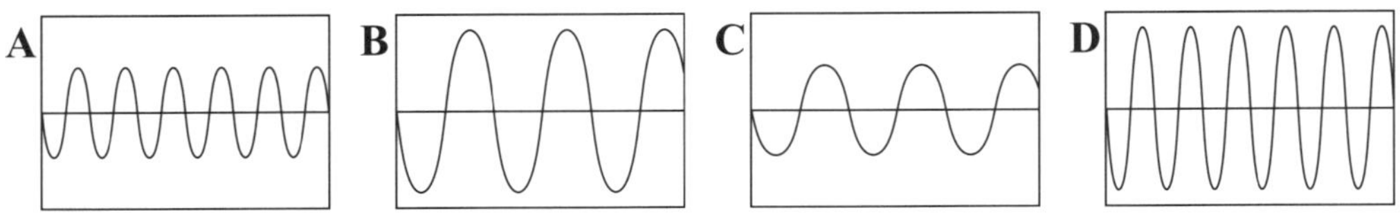

(a) Write the letters of the alarm sounds in the correct boxes in the table below.

	60 dB	80 dB
8000 Hz		
10 000 Hz		

(b) What property of a sound wave is measured in

(i) hertz (Hz)? ....

(ii) decibels (dB)? ....

(c) Tom knows that he needs a louder,
higher-pitched alarm sound to wake up.
Which sound should he choose, A, B, C or D? ....

(d) (i) The sound is created and travels to Tom as vibrations.
Write down the letters to give the order in which they vibrate.

A hairs in the cochlea **B** loudspeaker **C** ear drum **D** air **E** ear bones

1 .... 2 .... 3 .... 4 .... 5 ....

(ii) What happens to the vibrations so that Tom's brain is able to turn them into the sound of his alarm?

....

....

(e) Tom puts the clock on the far side of his bedside table.
Explain why it would be better to put the clock on the near side of the table.

....

Light and Sound Mini-Exam — Part Two

2 The Ancient Greek philosopher Aristotle thought that neither sound nor light could travel through a vacuum.

The diagram shows one of the first experiments carried out by scientists to test this idea. All the air was pumped out of the bell jar, creating a vacuum.

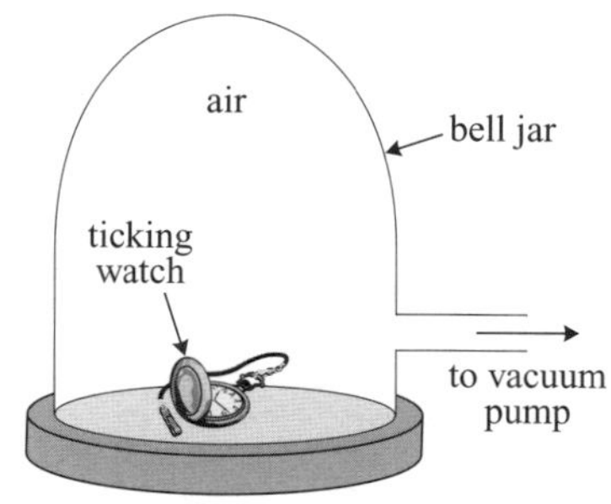

(a) (i) If Aristotle was correct and both sound and light were unable to travel through a vacuum, what would the scientists have expected to observe?

....

....

(ii) What did the scientists actually observe?

....

(b) What did the result tell scientists

(i) about sound? ....

(ii) about light? ....

3 A device called an **echo sounder** can be used by ships to find objects underwater. This device sends pulses of sound into the ocean and detects any echo from an object. The time it takes for the pulse to come back gives the distance to the object. Below are three oscilloscope traces of pulses from an echo sounder.

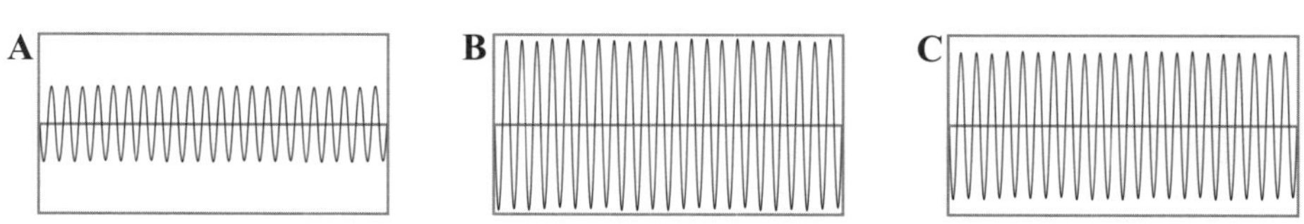

(a) Which trace **best** represents the pulse

(i) When it is first sent out? ....

(ii) When it comes back after 1 second? ....

(iii) When it comes back after 3 seconds? ....

(b) Explain your answer to (a).

....

Day and Night

1 The diagram on the right shows the Earth.
The city of Kuala Lumpur in Malaysia is labelled KL.

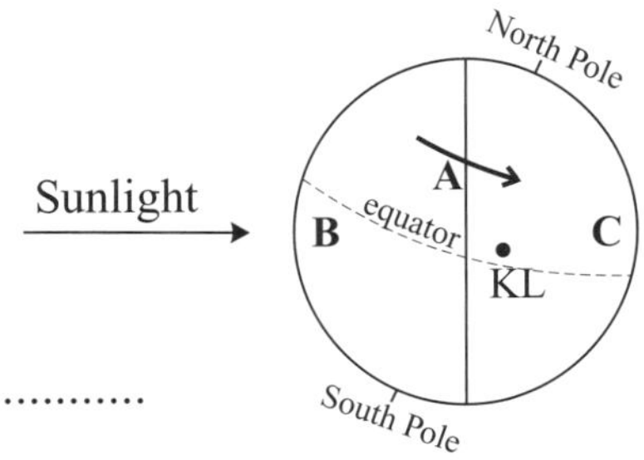

(a) (i) On the diagram, what is shown by the arrow **A**?

....

(ii) A day lasts twenty-four hours. What happens to the Earth during this time?

....

(b) Look at regions **B** and **C** on the diagram, and say whether it is daytime or night time at each.

....

(c) Tick the statement that **best** describes the time of day in Kuala Lumpur.

- ☐ **It is midday.**
- ☐ **The Sun has just set.**
- ☐ **The Sun will rise soon.**
- ☐ **It is midnight.**

2 The diagram below shows the path of the Sun across the sky for one day in winter.

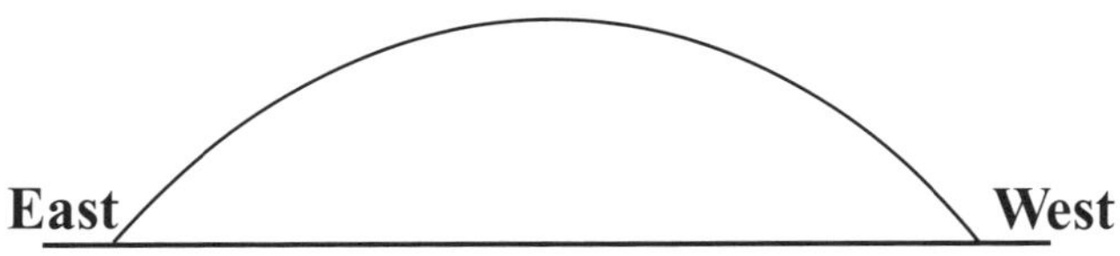

(a) (i) Mark the position of the Sun at midday with a cross.

(ii) Draw an arrow on the path to show the direction the Sun appears to move in.

(iii) Draw the path of the Sun across the sky for one day in summer.
Label the path **summer**, and mark the position of the Sun at midday with a cross.

(b) Are shadows at midday longest during **winter** or **summer**? Explain your answer.

....

....

The Seasons

1 The diagram below shows the Earth at four points in its orbit around the Sun.

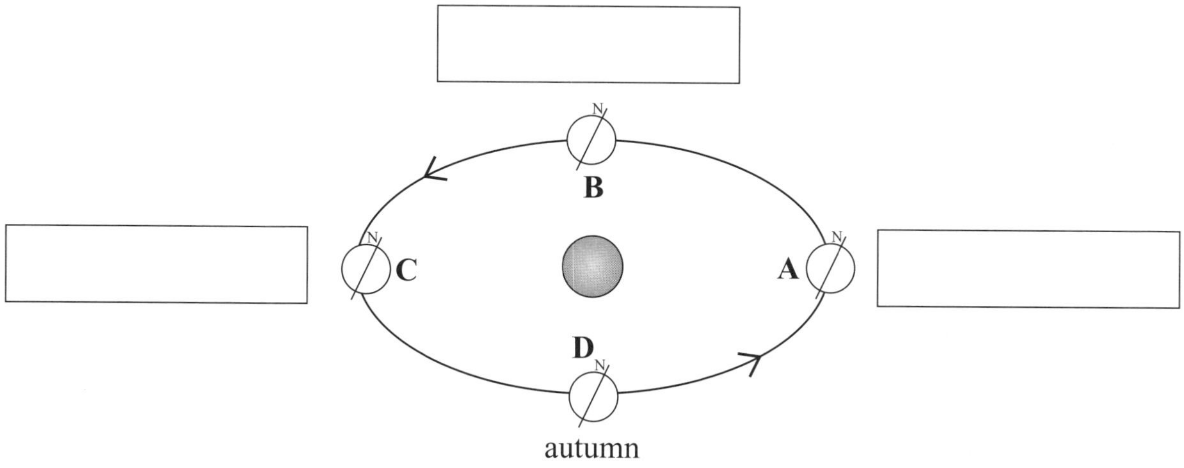

(a) Fill in the missing labels on the diagram to show all four seasons in the northern hemisphere.

(b) How long will it take the Earth to move from position A to position B, in months?

....

(c) Cross out **four** words so that the sentences below are correct.

At position C, the northern half of the Earth has longer / shorter days than nights and the Sun's rays spread over a larger / smaller area of land. The heating effect of the Sun is at its strongest / weakest and it gets warm / cold.

(d) What causes the seasons? Tick the correct box.

☐ **The Earth rotates on its axis.**

☐ **The Earth moves closer to the Sun at certain times of year.**

☐ **The height of the midday Sun changes depending on the time of year.**

☐ **The Earth's axis leans over at an angle of 23.5°.**

Satellites

1 The Moon is usually the brightest object in the night sky.

(a) Fill in the gaps in the following sentences about the Moon.

The Moon is the Earth's only .... satellite.

It moves in .... direction around the Earth,

completing one orbit every .... days.

The diagram on the right shows the Moon at different points in its orbit around the Earth.

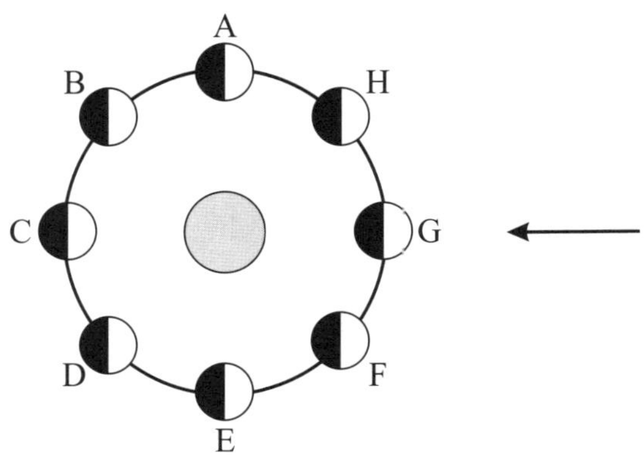

(b) (i) What does the arrow in the diagram represent?

....

....

(ii) Explain how we are able to see the Moon from the Earth, even though it has no light of its own.

....

(c) The Moon appears to change shape as it orbits the Earth.

(i) Match each of the following views of the Moon from the Earth with **one** of the positions **A** to **H** in the diagram above.

Position ....

Position ....

Position ....

Position ....

(ii) Explain why the Moon appears to change shape as it orbits the Earth.

....

Gravity

1 Satellites are kept in orbit by a force of attraction.

(a) What is the name of the force that keeps satellites in orbit?

....

The diagram below shows the Earth and the Moon, and two imaginary planets and moons. All the moons have the same mass and all the planets have the same density.

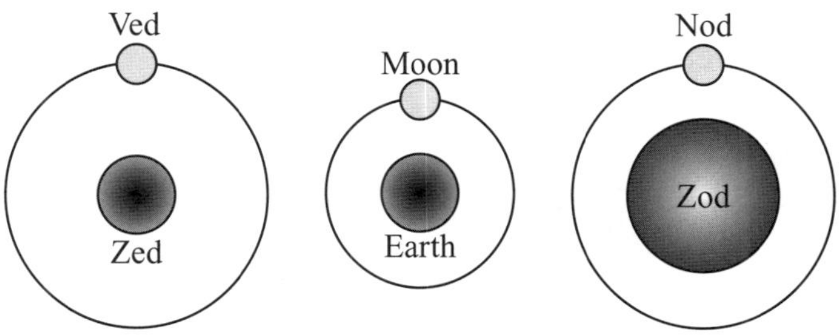

(b) Nod orbits at the same distance from Zod as the Moon orbits from the Earth. Is the force of attraction between Nod and Zod **smaller**, **larger** or **the same** as the force of attraction between the Earth and the Moon? Explain your answer.

....

....

(c) Zed has the same mass as the Earth. Is the force of attraction between Zed and Ved **smaller**, **larger** or **the same** as the force of attraction between the Earth and the Moon? Explain your answer.

....

....

(d) A probe is sent from the Earth to land on Zod and explore it.

(i) How will the **mass** of the probe on Zod compare to its mass on the Earth?

....

(ii) How will the **weight** of the probe on Zod compare to its weight on the Earth? Explain your answer.

....

....

Artificial Satellites

1 The diagram below shows a communications satellite.
Stations on the ground transmit and receive signals from the satellite.

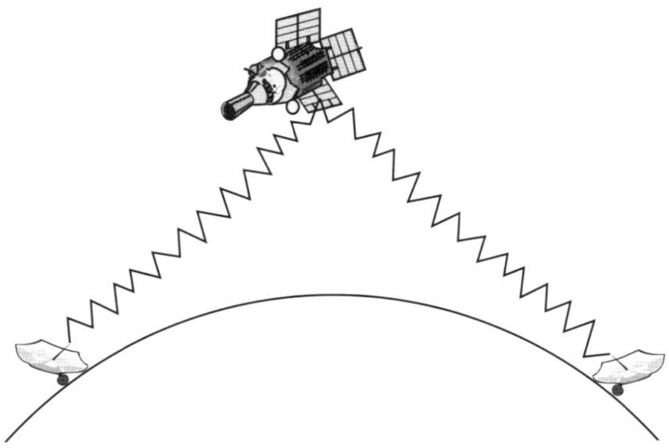

(a) What might signals sent by the satellite be used for? Give **two** examples.

1 .... 2 ....

(b) What is the advantage of using a satellite instead of sending signals between stations on the ground?

....

(c) The satellite completes one orbit for every rotation of the Earth.
This is called a geostationary orbit. Suggest what is meant by **geostationary**.

....

2 Scientists use artificial satellites to gather information.

(a) The Hubble Space Telescope is used to observe the Universe.
Explain why it has a much clearer view than telescopes on the Earth's surface.

....

(b) Describe **one** way that scientists use artificial satellites to gather information about the Earth.

....

The Solar System

1 The planets in the Solar System orbit around the Sun, which is a star.

(a) (i) List the following objects in the Solar System in order of **size**, smallest first.

Neptune **Earth** **Sun** **Pluto** **Jupiter**

.... **smallest**

....

....

....

.... **largest**

(ii) Explain why everything in the Solar System is kept in orbit around the Sun.

....

....

(b) Explain why the planets in the Solar System are visible from Earth, even though they don't give out light.

....

(c) (i) Why are Mercury, Venus, Earth and Mars known as the **inner planets**?

....

(ii) Draw lines to match each of the planets below with its distance from the Sun.

Planet	**Average distance from the Sun (millions of km)**
Mars	1430
Saturn	150
Earth	228
Uranus	2870

(d) Name **one** other type of object in the Solar System, apart from stars and planets.

....

The Solar System

1 The table on the right contains information about the planets in our Solar System.

Planet	Relative size	Relative mass
Earth	1.0	1.0
Jupiter	11.0	318.0
Mars	0.5	0.1
Mercury	0.4	0.05
Neptune	3.8	17.0
Pluto	0.2	0.003
Saturn	9.4	95.0
Uranus	4.0	15.0
Venus	0.9	0.8

(a) What does the word **relative** tell you about the values for size and mass given in the table?

....

....

....

(b) (i) Which of the planets is most like Earth in both **size** and **mass**?

....

(ii) Which planet is the third largest in **size**?

....

(iii) Which planet is the third largest in **mass**?

....

2 Below is a **simplified** diagram of the orbits of Venus, Earth, Mars and Jupiter, and a table showing their orbit times to the nearest half year.

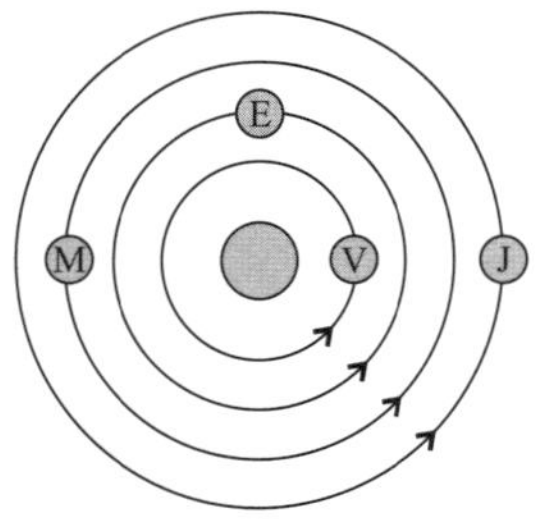

Planet	Orbit time (Earth years)
Venus	0.5
Earth	1.0
Mars	2.0
Jupiter	12.0

(a) Describe the relationship between a planet's distance from the Sun and its orbit time.

....

(b) Give **one** way in which the orbits shown in the diagram are simplified.

....

....

Beyond the Solar System

1 The most distant object that can be seen from the Earth without using a telescope is a galaxy called **Andromeda**.

(a) Write down the following objects in order of size, smallest first.

Sun **Solar System** **Universe** **Earth** **a galaxy**

.... **smallest**

....

....

....

.... **largest**

(b) What is a galaxy?

....

(c) Describe what Andromeda looks like from the Earth.

....

....

(d) There are several different types of galaxies.
Our own galaxy is usually described as a **spiral** galaxy.

(i) What is our own galaxy called?

....

(ii) There are other spiral galaxies in the Universe, but from Earth they look like single stars, not spirals. Why is this?

....

....

The Earth and Beyond Mini-Exam

1 The diagram below shows the Earth orbiting the Sun. The diagram is not drawn to scale.

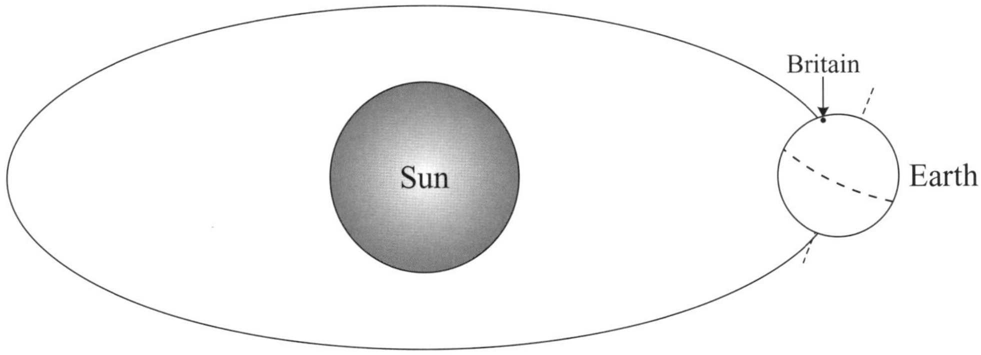

(a) What term is used to describe the **shape** of the Earth's orbit? Tick the correct box.

☐ **circular** ☐ **ovaloid**

☐ **elliptical** ☐ **rounded**

(b) What is the time taken to complete one orbit known as?

....

As it orbits, the Earth rotates on its axis, causing day and night.

(c) On the diagram above

(i) label the Earth's **axis**.

(ii) shade one half of the Earth to show which region is in night time.

(d) What **two** other effects does the Earth's rotation have? Tick the correct boxes.

☐ **The Sun rises and sets every day.**

☐ **The Moon appears to change shape as it orbits the Earth.**

☐ **The height of the Sun at midday changes.**

☐ **The stars follow curved paths through the night sky.**

The Earth and Beyond Mini-Exam

(e) Look at the position of Britain in the diagram at the beginning of the question.

(i) Which statement below is true for Britain? Tick the correct box.

☐ **Daytime lasts longer than night time.**

☐ **Night time lasts longer than daytime.**

(ii) In Britain, will the heating effect of the Sun be at its **strongest** or **weakest**? Explain your answer.

....

....

(iii) In the diagram, what season is it in Britain?

....

(iv) What season will it be in the southern half of the Earth? Explain your answer.

....

....

(f) If the diagram at the start of the question was drawn to scale, how should the Sun be drawn if the Earth was left the same size? Tick the correct box.

☐ **much smaller** ☐ **slightly smaller**

☐ **slightly larger** ☐ **much larger**

(g) Earth orbits a very small area of the Solar System in which life can be sustained.

(i) Suggest which **two** planets orbit just outside this area.

1 .... 2 ....

(ii) Suggest why life cannot be sustained on these two planets.

1 ....

2 ....

The Earth and Beyond Mini-Exam

2 Mars has two moons. Many scientists think that these moons are asteroids that became trapped in orbit around Mars.

(a) Cross out **three** words so that the following sentences about Mars are correct.

Mars is the second / fourth planet from the Sun, the last of the inner planets. It is half / twice the size of the Earth and has a year 225 / 687 days long.

(b) What feature of the Solar System lies between Mars and the outer planets, that might help to explain where Mars' moons came from?

....

(c) The moons can be described as satellites of Mars. Explain what a **satellite** is.

....

(d) (i) What force of attraction would have trapped the moons in orbit around Mars?

....

(ii) What causes this force of attraction between Mars and its moons?

....

3 **Comets** travel right to the edges of the Solar System. They are thought to be like giant, dirty snowballs. The diagram on the right shows the orbit of one comet around the Sun. As it gets near to the Sun it melts, and a 'tail' of gas and dust is formed.

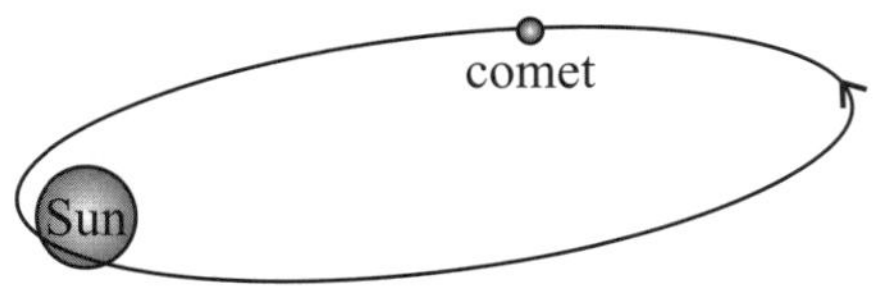

(a) (i) What type of object is the Sun? ....

(ii) Suggest what causes the comet to melt as it gets near to the Sun.

....

(b) What will happen to the **gravity** affecting the comet as it gets closer to the Sun? Explain your answer.

....

....

The Earth and Beyond Mini-Exam

4 The diagram on the right shows the stars in the constellation Orion.

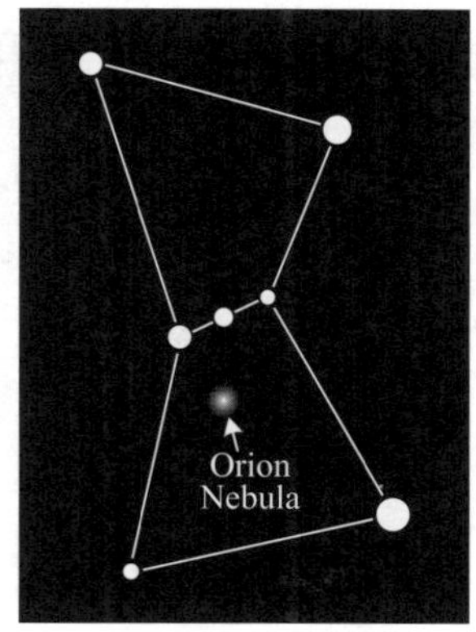

(a) Seen from the Earth, the stars in Orion appear to be close to each other and all moving in the same direction. In fact, they are not related. Suggest **one** reason why they appear to be a group when seen from the Earth.

....

....

(b) One of the objects in Orion, called the **Orion Nebula**, is not really a star. It looks dim and blurred compared to the stars in the constellation.

(i) Suggest what type of object the Orion Nebula might be.

....

(ii) Explain why this type of object appears blurred when seen from the Earth.

....

5 The diagram on the right shows two artificial satellites in orbit around the Earth. Satellite A orbits round the poles and satellite B orbits round the equator.

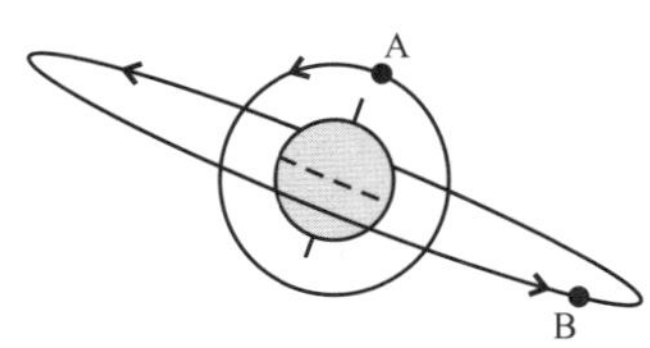

(a) The satellites are travelling at the same speed, and have orbit times of 2 and 24 hours. Which one has the orbit time of 24 hours, **A** or **B**? Explain your answer.

....

....

(b) One satellite is a weather satellite and the other is a television satellite. Which is likely to be which? Give a reason for your answers.

Satellite .... **is likely to be the weather satellite because** ....

....

Satellite .... **is likely to be the television satellite because** ....

....

Forms of Energy

1 Different forms of energy are needed for different activities.

(a) Write down the **main** form of energy being demonstrated in each of the pictures below.

(i)  ....

(iii)  ....

(ii)  ....

(iv)  ....

(b) Draw lines to join each form of energy on the left to its **most appropriate** example on the right.

chemical	**digging the garden**
sound	**a skydiver stepping out of an aeroplane**
gravitational potential	**a bar of chocolate**
kinetic	**loud music on the radio**

(c) A simplified diagram of an electrical circuit used in a car is shown below. Complete the table to show the main form of energy in each component.

Component	Form of energy
Battery	
Wires	
Starter motor	
Headlamp	
Radio loudspeaker	

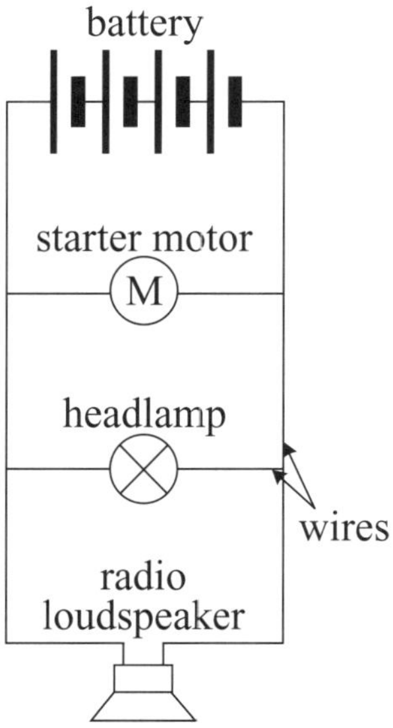

Forms of Energy

1 Look at the list below.

A	gravitational	**E**	thermal
B	light	**F**	elastic
C	chemical	**G**	electrical
D	temperature		

(a) Which item in the list is **not** a form of energy? Write down the correct letter.

....

(b) Which item gives another name for heat energy? Write down the correct letter.

....

(c) Which form of energy is given out by **luminous** objects?
Write down the correct letter.

....

(d) Which form of energy in the list is found wherever there is a current flowing?
Write down the correct letter.

....

(e) Which **three** items in the list are forms of stored energy?
Write down the correct letters and give an example for each one.

Letter .... **Example** ....

....

Letter .... **Example** ....

....

Letter .... **Example** ....

....

Energy Transformations

1 The picture shows a radio powered by solar cells.

(a) What energy transformation happens in the solar cells?

.... → ....

(b) What energy transformation happens in the radio's speaker?

.... → ....

(c) Will all of the energy gained by the solar cells be given out by the speaker? Explain your answer.

....

....

2 An electric toothbrush has a rechargeable battery.

(a) What energy transformation takes place when the battery is recharged? Tick the correct box.

☐ **Kinetic to sound** ☐ **Electrical to chemical**

☐ **Chemical to electrical** ☐ **Heat to kinetic**

(b) What **useful** energy transformation takes place when the toothbrush is used? Tick the correct box.

☐ **Electrical to kinetic to sound** ☐ **Electrical to chemical to kinetic**

☐ **Chemical to electrical to kinetic** ☐ **Chemical to sound to kinetic**

(c) Write down **two** forms in which energy is **wasted** when the toothbrush is used.

1 .... 2 ....

Energy Transformations

1 Joss is hammering a nail into a wall.

(a) The energy of the hammer comes from energy stored in Joss's muscles.

(i) What form was this energy stored in?

....

(ii) Where did Joss get this energy?

....

(iii) The stored energy is transformed when Joss uses the hammer.
What form of energy does it become?

....

(b) Some of the hammer's energy is transferred to the nail, making it move into the wall, and some is wasted.

(i) What form of energy is the **useful** energy transferred by the hammer?

....

(ii) Suggest **two** forms in which the hammer's energy is **wasted**.

1 .... 2 ....

2 Write down the energy transformations happening in the pictures below.
(Note that energy can be converted into **more than one** form.)

(a)

....

....

(b)

....

....

Energy Resources

1 Plants convert light energy from the Sun into other forms, providing us with energy resources in the form of **biomass**.

(a) What process takes place when a plant converts light energy from the Sun?

....

(b) (i) Name **one** type of biomass we use as an energy resource.

....

(ii) For the type of biomass named in (i), describe the chain of energy transformations that converts energy from the Sun into a form that we use.

....

....

....

(c) Apart from biomass, what other energy resource is provided by plants? Tick the correct box.

☐ **tidal power** ☐ **wind power**

☐ **fossil fuels** ☐ **geothermal power**

2 Wind turbines can be used to generate electricity from the wind.

(a) What form of energy does the wind have?

....

(b) Where does the wind's energy come from? Explain your answer.

....

....

(c) What other energy resource results from the wind?

....

Generating Electricity

1 The diagram below shows the process by which electricity is generated in a power station.

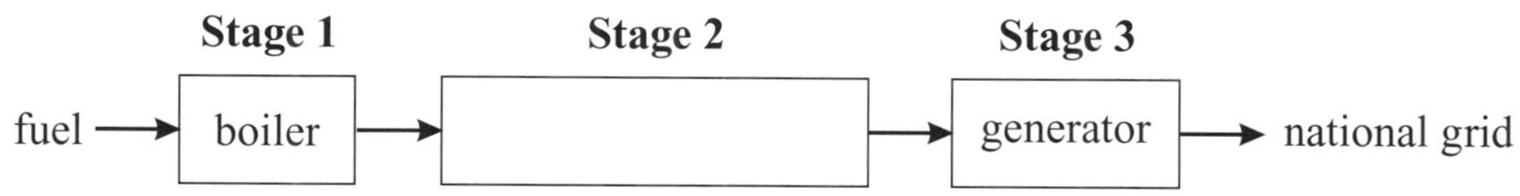

(a) Fill in the missing label to show what piece of equipment stage 2 takes place in.

(b) At which stage do the following events happen?
Write down the correct number for each one.

(i) **Kinetic energy is converted into electrical energy** at stage ....

(ii) **The force of steam at high pressure drives rotating blades** at stage ....

(iii) **Chemical energy is converted into heat energy** at stage ....

(iv) **Rotation is used to produce an electric current** at stage ....

(v) **Heat energy becomes kinetic energy** at stage ....

(vi) **Water is heated to make steam** at stage ....

(c) (i) Name **three** fossil fuels which are burnt in power stations.

1 .... 2 ....

3 ....

(ii) Explain why petrol is **not** a fuel burnt in power stations.

....

(d) Explain what the **national grid** does.

....

....

Generating Electricity

1 Scientists have warned that supplies of fossil fuels will eventually run out.

(a) The natural processes that lead to the formation of fossil fuels are always going on. Explain why these fuels will run out.

....

....

(b) Why is it particularly important to reduce the rate at which we are burning **oil**? Tick the correct box.

☐ **Burning oil can lead to explosions.**

☐ **Oil has many important uses other than generating electricity.**

☐ **Burning oil releases more harmful chemicals into the environment than burning other fossil fuels does.**

(c) The amount of fossil fuels burnt can be reduced by **using less energy** and by using **renewable energy resources** instead.

(i) Suggest **two** ways of using less energy.

1 ....

2 ....

(ii) Name **three** renewable energy resources that could be used to replace fossil fuels.

1 ....

2 ....

3 ....

Conservation of Energy

1 The energy transformations that take place in a hair dryer are shown below.

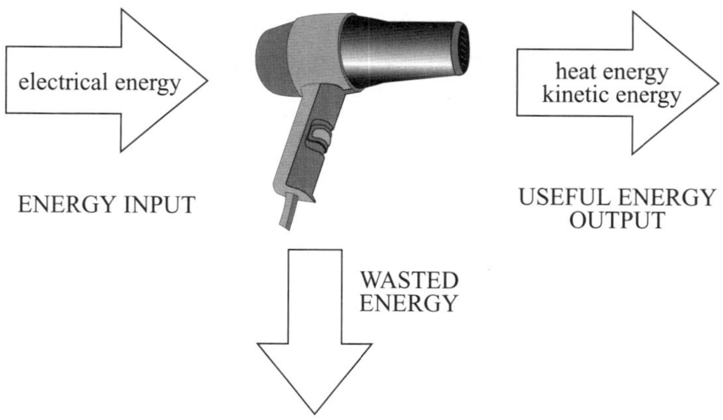

(a) (i) What type of energy is wasted by the hair dryer?

....

(ii) Explain why this energy is described as **wasted**.

....

....

(b) Tick the equation that is correct for the hair dryer shown above.

☐ **wasted energy + electrical energy = useful energy output**

☐ **heat energy + kinetic energy = energy input – wasted energy**

☐ **electrical energy = wasted energy + heat energy**

☐ **wasted energy = heat energy + kinetic energy – energy input**

(c) Shanaz states that the hair dryer "uses up energy".
Explain why this statement is incorrect.

....

....

Conservation of Energy

1 Look at the pictures of the two light bulbs.
The ordinary light bulb has an energy input of 100 joules per second.
The energy saver light bulb has an energy input of 20 joules per second.
Both bulbs give out the same amount of light energy per second.

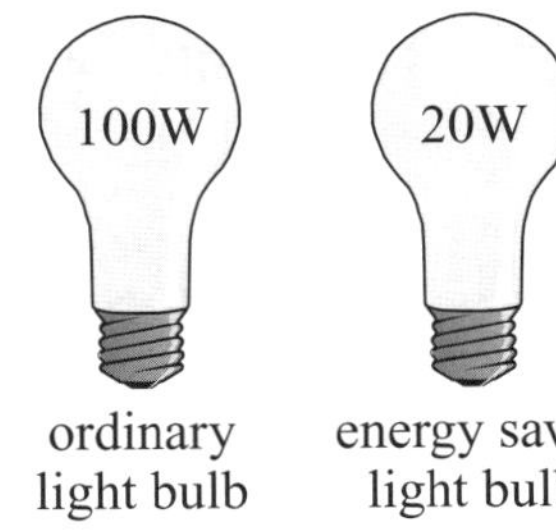

(a) Explain how it is possible that both bulbs can give out the same amount of light energy per second.

....

(b) Suggest **two** advantages of using the energy saver bulbs instead of the ordinary bulbs.

1 ....

2 ....

2 A petrol-engined car, electric lawnmower and wind turbine all waste energy at different rates.

(a) Calculate the following energy values for each device.

(i) For every 100 joules of energy input, the car wastes 75 joules.

Useful energy = ... **joules**

(ii) For every 80 joules of useful energy output, the lawnmower wastes 120 joules.

Input energy = ... **joules**

(iii) The wind turbine has an energy input of 400 joules and an energy output of 80 joules.

Wasted energy = ... **joules**

(b) What is the **useful** form of energy output by:

(i) both the car and the lawnmower? ....

(ii) the wind turbine? ....

(c) Which device is

(i) **most** wasteful of energy? ....

(ii) **least** wasteful of energy? ....

(d) Name **two** forms of energy wasted by all three devices.

1 .... 2 ....

Energy Resources and Energy Mini-Exam

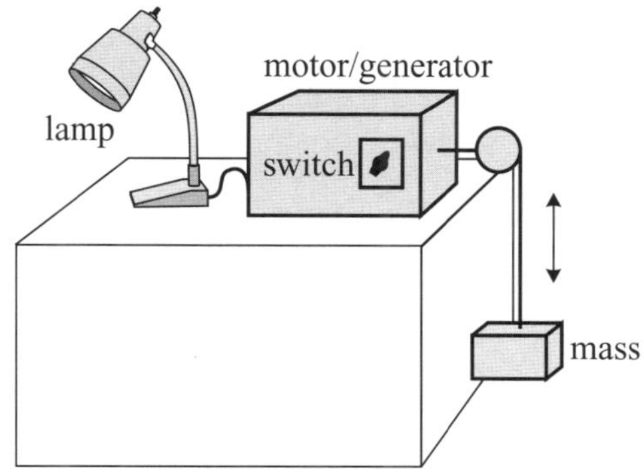

1 The device shown in the diagram on the right contains a battery-powered motor. When the motor is switched on, it raises the mass. When it is switched off, the mass falls. This drives the generator, which makes the lamp light.

(a) When the motor is switched on, energy is transferred from the motor's battery to the mass.

(i) Fill in the spaces below to show the **useful** energy transformations that take place in the battery and motor as the mass is lifted.

	battery →		**motor** →	
....		....		....
energy		**energy**		**energy**

(ii) The energy is now stored in the mass. What form is the energy stored in?

....

(b) (i) What energy transformation takes place in the mass as it falls?

....

(ii) Complete the diagram below to show the **useful** energy transformations that take place in the generator and the lamp as the mass falls.

	generator →		**lamp** →	
....		....		....
energy		**energy**		**energy**

(iii) What form of **wasted** energy is given out by the lamp?

....

(c) How will the amount of energy given out by the **lamp** compare to the amount of energy given out by the **battery**? Explain your answer.

....

....

....

Energy Resources and Energy Mini-Exam

2 Pete and Alice have two ways of heating their house. They can burn oil in a boiler connected to the central heating system, and they can burn wood in their kitchen stove.

Look at the list of energy resources below.

A	Biomass	**C**	Geothermal
B	Solar	**D**	Fossil fuels

(a) (i) What type of energy resource is oil an example of?
Write down the correct letter.

....

(ii) Give **two** other examples of this type of energy resource.

1 .... 2 ....

(b) (i) What type of energy resource is wood an example of?
Write down the correct letter.

....

(ii) Give **one** other example of this type of energy resource.

....

(c) (i) Explain why the **Sun** is important in the production of oil and wood.

....

(ii) Explain why **photosynthesis** is important in the production of oil and wood.

....

....

(iii) Explain how the formation of oil is different from the formation of wood.

....

....

....

Energy Resources and Energy Mini-Exam

(d) Complete the diagram below to show the chain of energy transformations that take place to provide Pete and Alice with a warm house.

....	⟶	....	**burning** ⟶	....
energy		**energy**		**energy**

(e) When Pete and Alice burn the wood and oil

(i) is **energy** being used up? Explain your answer.

....

....

(ii) are **energy resources** being used up? Explain your answer.

....

....

(f) Alice says that they should use the boiler less and use the stove more because "wood is an example of a renewable energy resource and oil is not".

(i) Explain why wood is a renewable energy resource and oil is a non-renewable energy resource.

....

....

....

(ii) Give **one** reason why scientists warn that we should reduce the rate at which we are burning fuels like oil.

....

....

(iii) Name **two** other renewable energy resources, apart from wood.

1 ....

2 ....

Energy Resources and Energy Mini-Exam

3 Agnes is using a food mixer. The electricity supplied to the mixer is mostly generated in power stations burning fossil fuels.

(a) The table below shows the machines used to generate electricity in a fossil fuel power station, and the energy transformation that happens in each machine.

	Machine	Energy Transformation
A	generator	
B		heat to kinetic
C	boiler	

(i) Complete the table by filling in the missing information.

(ii) Write down the letters of the machines to show the order in which they are used to generate electricity.

....

(b) As shown in the diagram below, energy is lost when the electricity is generated, when it is transported to Agnes's home and when the food mixer is used.

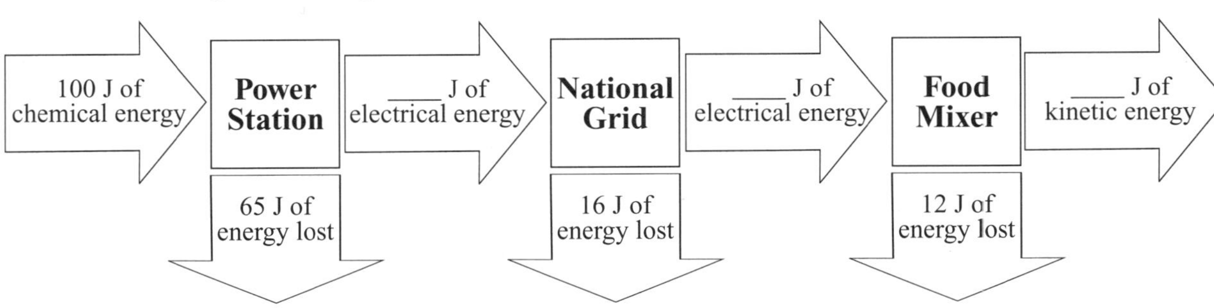

(i) In what form is energy usually lost?

....

(ii) Look at the diagram. How much energy is lost as the electricity is transported to Agnes's home?

....

(iii) Complete the diagram to show how much useful energy is given out by the power station, National Grid and food mixer for every 100 J of energy in the fuel burnt by the power stations.